THE RAPE OF FATIMAH

— *or* —

WORL' DO FOR FRAID

A Play in Three Acts,
with Music

by

Nabie Yayah Swaray

Africa World Press, Inc.

P.O. Box 1892
Trenton, NJ 08607

P.O. Box 48
Asmara, ERITREA

Africa World Press, Inc.

P.O. Box 1892 P.O. Box 48
Trenton, NJ 08607 Asmara, ERITREA

Book design: Saverance Publishing Services
                    (www.saverancepublishing.com)
Cover design: Ashraful Haque
Cover art: Rebecca Bailey

Library of Congress Cataloging-in-Publication Data

Swaray, Nabie Yayah.
 [Worl' do for fraid]
 The rape of Fatimah, or, Worl' do for fraid : a play in three acts, with music / by Nabie Yayah Swaray.
     p. cm.
 Originally published: Worl' do for fraid. Washington, D.C. : Three Continents Press, 1986.
 ISBN 1-59221-656-0 (cloth) -- ISBN 1-59221-657-9 (pbk.)
 1. Sierra Leone--Drama. I. Title. II. Title: Rape of Fatimah. III. Title: Worl' do for fraid.

PR9393.9.S93W6 2008
822'.92--dc22

                              2008029993

Dedicated to my mother —
Mariama N'turay Swaray

Table of Contents

Preface

This fine first play of Nabie Swaray's does what any considerable play must: it makes of the facts of experience that larger
use of them than social scientists or journalists do, which, like
it or not, we must call myth, an arrangement of men moving
to life's chances which may convey true news of our common
humanity. This play initiates us into the chaos, which pre-
cedes creation, the chaos which in newspaper expositions of it
seems mere disorder. Its unfolding initiates us into the mixed
motives of superstitious reserve, bewildered longing and terrified reason which bedevil the play's characters, as the people
around them, their government, and their very locale change
into something unrecognizable. Swaray has a motherlode of
ideas to mine, prodigious energy and drive, and unique insight into a world largely closed to Western eyes. In potential,
he is another Wole Soyinka.

William Alfred
A.L.Lowell Professor of Humanities
Harvard University

Foreword

A continent whose largely unexplored interior appeared mysterious and magical to Europeans, Africa was once dubbed "the Dark Continent" by Henry Morton Stanley (1841-1904) in his documented explorations chronicled in *Through the Dark Continent* (1877). This myth and stereotype of Africa by a European are further reinforced and articulated by Joseph Conrad (1857-1924) in a most negative portrait painted in his novel *Heart of Darkness* (1899/1902), where the protagonist goes on an adventure to the Congo Free State. These publications depict authorial bias, for the creators of the texts are writing as observers of African culture, not with the expertise and insider knowledge of the native eye.

These Victorian era prejudices, stereotypes, and myths about Africa that depict the continent as shrouded and eclipsed in total darkness have found their way into Western literature. However, Africa as "the Dark Continent" based on the observations of Henry Morton Stanley and Joseph Conrad writing about Africa has been challenged and exposed by contemporary African writers, such as Camara Laye (1928-80), author of the novel *The African Child/The Dark Child* (1953); Chinua Achebe (b. 1930), author of the novel *Things Fall Apart*

(1958); and Wole Soyinka (b. 1934), author of the play *Death and the King's Horseman* (1975). These twentieth century African writers presented a picture of Africa that is based on the authenticity of African culture as experienced and observed by natives of the continent. They endeavored in their writings, moreover, to present to non-African readers a true portrait of Africa as a continent that is far removed from Henry Morton Stanley's and Joseph Conrad's universally accepted portrait of pre-colonial and early colonial Africa. With the emergence of African literature by indigenous writers, the African continent is still an unconquered territory whose interior remains mysterious and magical to Europe, America, Asia, and other parts of the world. The authenticity of Africa as presented in African literature is augmented by the accepted notion that African literary beginnings are rich in oral traditions, customs, and beliefs. Hence, the early written literature of Africa by Africans is indebted to the oral tradition and its storytelling genres, such as folktales, poetry, proverbs, riddles, songs, dance, legends, myths, and the griot, i.e., the recorder of the past, the severe critic of the present, the prophesier of the future, and the preserver of institutions. With the lifting of the veil on Africa's land, people, and customs, a new era is born that begins an explosion of twentieth century contemporary literature with indigenous Africans producing creative works in African and European languages. These African writers, painters, sculptors, and other artists now provide the unexplored and more-to-be-explored interior layers and territory of Africa's richest legacy of traditions, customs, beliefs, and philosophies.

A prolific group of talented African writers has produced literature using narrative and poetry as expressions relating the racial indignities suffered at the hands of European oppressors, as well as the disintegration of African traditions. Nigerian writers Amos Tutuola (1920-97), who wrote *The Palm-Wine Drinkard* (1952), and Chinua Achebe, who wrote *Things Fall Apart*, the representative example of the archetypal African novel, are among the African novelists who have garnered international fame. In addition, African playwrights have used the art form of dramatic production to depict African cultural, economic, historical, political, and social conflicts and to revitalize African indigenous languages and songs. Nobel Laureate for Literature in 1986, Wole Soyinka, achieved international recognition for his voluminous body of work and for his plays, such as *Death and the King's Horseman*. Nabie Yayah Swaray (b. 1953) joined the ranks of influential African playwrights at Harvard and The Writers' Workshop at the University of Iowa where he honed his skills. His first play *Dance of the Witches* had a public reading during his initial year at Harvard. Swaray's second play, *The Drums of Death* (1976), retitled *Worl' Do for Fraid*, also had a public reading at Cambridge's Dudley House Drama Club and the New African Company at Lehman Hall in 1978. It was presented in live performance by the Boston Arts Group in 1980 in Boston and at Cambridge in 1984. He is a prodigious playwright, creating a portfolio of impressive dramatic works. The setting of *Worl' Do for Fraid or the Rape of Fatimah* is Kissy Mess-Mess, a suburb of Freetown, Sierra Leone. The play begins in July 1950 during the rainy season and covers a time frame of approximately one month.

The play's characters reveal complex issues that plague Kissy Mess-Mess and the Bangura family. Drissa, the village chief, and Baimbadi, his twin brother and co-ruler, are the epitome of endemic corruption. The two of them in a conspiratorial alliance rape a virtuous young woman, the chief's adopted daughter, in the name of an Islamic prophesy to gain political power. The emotional scarring of the young woman is inconsequential to their conscience. To rule justly or unjustly, to be held in high esteem, and to be important male heads of their families are the only concerns central to their worldview. They elevate their criminal involvement when they murder Makalay and Abbi, Drissa's wife and daughter, for fear that their sadistic act and unlawful killing will be publicly exposed. Baimbadi's morally degenerate behavior compels him to cover up the rape of the chief's adopted daughter and present her as a virgin in the proposed marriage ceremony. A coalition of secrecy surrounds them, but old world traditions performed by Baimbadi's wife help to expose their ungodliness and revenge the innocent. *A Man of the People* (1966) by Chinua Achebe satirizes political corruption in a manner similar to Swaray's depiction of the corrupt brothers.

Saidu and Abass are the first and second born sons of Baimbadi and Nene. They are ultra opposites, Saidu remaining in the village and adhering to the traditional ways and Abass going abroad to pursue a European education. Abass returns after a ten-year absence, only to become disillusioned by his brother's lack of productivity and career goals and the village's lapse into a stagnant time machine, maintaining religious and ritual practices that are dying forms irrelevant to post-colonial times. On the one hand, Saidu, representing indigenous traditional practices, agrees to an arranged marriage to Fatimah. As the prospective groom, he asserts his masculine authority over Fatimah, ordering her about, for the engagement period announces them as a married pair awaiting a public ceremonial presence to sanction the union. He has no real vocation; he is the son of a powerful man. On the other hand, Abass represents change. He has national loyalty, choosing to use his medical degree in his homeland rather than in England; he has acquired higher education so that he will have a meaningful medical career working at the local hospital; but he has little tolerance for animism, Islam, or Christianity. His views from his newly acquired experiences clash with the traditions of his culture. The play's issue of cultural difference is treated comparably in *The African* (1960), a novel by William Conton (b. 1925) of Sierra Leone.

Pastor Brown, the family's confidant, is on a religious sojourn. He has experimented with Catholicism, Protestantism, Jehovah's Witness, and Baptist, finding no consolation with organized Western religion. His near-conversion to Islam emanated from the desire to become a polygamist. He settles down as a Bible carrying preacher who believes that Christ-like human suffering is par for the course of earthly inhabitants and that the infinite reward can only be acquired in the heavenly afterlife. He presents himself as the trusted friend of the Bangura family, encouraging them to confess verbally their inner most feelings, providing an opportunity for him to lead them in prayer or seize the moment to sermonize. Kenyan writer James Ngugi, also known as Ngugi wa Thiong'o (b. 1938), treats the impact of Christianity on African life in his various writings just as Swaray explores the issue in the play.

The comic relief character in the play is the market sweeper Pabuya. Although he provides humor through his speech and actions and sensitizes the audience to the scope of life and death through his role, he also speaks truthfully. Totally oblivious to the impending tragedy, he merely blurts out whatever his mind thinks. Ironically, an element of truth in his humorous mini soliloquies is an effective complex use of comic relief. Pabuya is also a festive drunk in the marriage scene, having in his possession a container of palm-wine. His character is reminiscent of Amos Tutuola's treatment of his drunken character in *The Palm-Wine Drinkard*.

Joshua and Brukus are friends of Abass who come to the Bangura compound to welcome him home. The three were former classmates under the tutelage of Pastor Brown. The friendship has survived a ten-year separation, and the two of them are the vehicle to reacquaint Abass with the culture. Through hospitality and healthy verbal exchange, Abass is gingerly re-instructed into the ways of a tribesman. Brukus is instrumental in detailing to Abass the explanation of dreams. Beneath reality is the existence of an unconscious, the graveyard of the unfulfilled desires of the conscious mind. However, Brukus alerts Abass that Sigmund Freud was ignorant about African interpretations of dreams. Brukus encourages Abass to bring his intellectual reasoning and his indigenous ritual practices to a peaceful compromise. An African poet who, like Swaray, explores life's conflicts and death's ominous presence is Kofi Awoonor (b. 1935) of Ghana.

Women in the play are dramatic representations in gender politics. Makalay is a ghost who was the wife of Drissa, mother of Abbi, and mother of Fatimah. Nene is the wife of Baimbadi and mother of Saidu and Abass. Makalay and Nene are twin sisters who marry twin brothers Drissa and Baimbadi.

xvi

Fatimah is the adopted daughter of Makalay and Drissa and the fiancée of Saidu. Godmamy presides over the wedding ceremony. The world of the women is pervasively patriarchal, and their anatomy restricts them in mobility and accomplishment. Domesticity is the world in which they reign, overseers of hearth, home, and marriage ceremony. Makalay cannot confront her husband regarding his evil deeds while she is alive, but in death she discovers her voice and assures her husband that she will avenge her and Abbi's premature expiration. Her boldness brings about Drissa's slow decline into mental unbalance and resultant death. Fatimah is the unfortunate victim of male dominance and control. A pathetic being who is drugged and sexually abused by pillars of the community who are her father figures, she owns nothing, not even her person. Because of the rape, she can no longer envision the greatness within her. She lacks voice, spunk, and courage, though she musters the fortitude to confess to Nene the awful event that robbed her of her innocence. Godmamy is the representation of "woman power," but it is a false representation. She is really complicit with masculine rule. Her role is to assure that the bridegroom gets a virgin, to use physical violence if necessary to get the bride to confess any indecent acts that contradict tradition. Nene is the character who breaks free of marginality and the masculine oppressive order. To acquire this authority, she challenges the categorization of womanhood, saying to her husband, "You think I'm only a woman, but you are wrong! You are a walking dead man." She is keenly aware of the need for a sisterhood, for women to unite and protect other women who are weak, fragile, and defenseless. She becomes the sole avenger of the violation of Fatimah. Through ancestor worship and ritual, Nene conjures the assistance of spirits to achieve justice for the weak and brokenhearted. Ama Ata Aidoo (b. 1942) writes about the role of African women in contemporary society. The women sections of the play can also be compared to Alice Walker's (b. 1944) *Possessing the Secret of Joy* (1992). Though not an African novelist, Walker has traveled widely in Africa and treats the African woman as subject from an African American point of view, giving focus to woman's voice and woman's alienation, as well as woman as survivor.

Like many contemporary African writers, Swaray incorporates into his creativity the literary traditions of the past. He possesses the insight to weave a storyline that reveals to the audience unknown aspects of African culture, thus deconstructing the myth and stereotype reinforced and articulated by European writers. Simultaneously, he is commentator on what is right and/or wrong with his homeland. In this manner, he follows in the pattern of the plays of Wole Soyinka, whose play *The Strong Breed* also examines the conflict between tribal tradition and contemporary change in Africa. There is so much that the West still does not understand about Africa, but playwrights like Swaray help to bring about cultural appreciation through creative endeavors.

Gerri Bates
Bowie State University

Gerri Bates, Coordinator of Africana Literature, teaches English, Africana literature, and Women's literature. She is the author of *Alice Walker: A Critical Companion* (Greenwood) and *The Color Purple: Character Studies* (Continuum).

Introduction

(*Lecture given at Agassiz House, Radcliffe College, Cambridge, Massachusetts, on May 19, 1984*)

I feel greatly honored to be asked by Mr. Swaray to offer some comments and observations on his play, *Worl' Do For Fraid*. I accept that invitation with great willingness, for I am enormously interested in the themes that he has set to dramatic form. It is an important play and we would do well to contemplate its message. I have discussed with him some of the ideas I would like to present here today, and since he did not then offer any serious resistance to my interpretations but in fact appears to concur at many significant points, I use that approval as my excuse for taking up the subject in the way I do.

I should in fact like to begin at the beginning, and suggest that, in addition to the literal translation of *Worl' Do For Fraid* as "this world is enough to frighten you," I would suggest that we interpret it as "it behooves us to be wary, for all our values and expectations are about to be shattered." The drum-roll of impending disaster is about to steal on our ears, and our understanding will be changed.

I propose, with your approval, to do three things in my remarks. Before presenting an outline of the play, I should like to provide some relevant background information concerning the history of Freetown and the pluralist religious world, in which it is immersed, the world of African religions, Islam and Christianity. I should next like to develop certain religious themes in an attempt to cast further light on some of the main characters in the play, and in this regard call attention to the special characteristics of the African tradition of religious inclusiveness with a corresponding communal openness to undergird that tradition. In my third and final stage, I should like to draw together several threads by concentrating on symbolic materials in the play, and dramatic tension of the characters, the elements of the stage scenes, the narrative power of the leading voices, and the bizarre fate that seems to mark the entire world-view of the play. I intend, as you can see, to spend the major portion of my time expounding the content of the play, with some interpretation.

The play opens in Kissy Mess Mess, which is in the east end of Freetown, Sierra Leone, a West African state that achieved independence in 1961, having been founded as a Christian settlement, initially of the "Black Poor" from London in 1787, and then of Afro-Americans, called in West Africa Nova Scotians, in 1792. As a Christian experiment, Freetown was an Afro-American achievement, and it was that legacy that was inherited by the "recaptives" of the early 19th century and subsequently transformed into a principle for the awakening of the African continent. In a major article describing the significance of the Afro-American factor in African Christianity, I called attention to the continuing repercussions of what was attempted and achieved in Freetown.

It is necessary only to summarize the main outlines of the historical and religious background to the play. Christianity arrived in Freetown in the hands of black preachers, many of whom were women. Eventually missionary superintendancy was asserted over the black congregations against much objection and resistance. Out of that explosive situation independent congregations were established, beginning in about 1820, led by the original black preachers or their successors. Their style of religion was what we today might call "open plan." They called it "revival religion," with its emphasis on spontaneity, personal fulfillment, lay leadership and congregational autonomy. For the purposes of the play, it is relevant to remark that "revival religion" unlike missionary Christianity, encouraged the recovery of ancient African religious practices, and that was the charge leveled against black preachers by an over-sensitive colonial Chaplaincy. The reliance on memory, rather than a set script, in preaching and exhortation shared a natural affinity with oral testimony in non-literate societies. As a consequence, possession by the Holy Spirit of the Bible was scarcely distinguishable from seizure by ancestor spirits or those of the local deities. Christian hymns, first begun to Western tunes, soon rose to heights of frenzy, bearing their singers to emotional peaks of ecstasy. The ministry of the word by preachers anointed with the availing force of Divine intervention evoked the oracles of ancient Africa where words, beginning in the consciousness like a calm trickle, would well up and gush out in cascades of reassurances. The identity between the two worlds was unmistakable, and officials were often intervening to stop a witch-trial of vengeance or break up a funeral wake keeping ceremony, in each case as an excess of the bounds of propriety. Abass, a character in the play, would have been an eager agent of official Freetown, for in that period, too, the catchword was for a wary vigilance in a world of strange goings-on.

The Islamic component in that world was just as firm. Islam had been present in Sierra Leone from a relatively early time. Muslim clerics were wandering into the Sierra Leone area from at least fifteenth century, following trade routes and being attracted to the small-organized political states in Susu country. Portuguese sources begin to identify such Muslim groups from the late 15th century, a period which coincided with the break-up of the Mali Empire created by Sunjata in 1237. Sierra Leone eventually became a neighboring corridor for the expansionist Islamized Fulbe of Futa Jallon, who, in 1727, created a theocratic state and planted satellite zones beyond the elevation of the plateau. One colonial governor in Freetown, Governor Rowe, for example, was highly regarded as a patron of visiting Muslims from Futa Jallon and in one instance he played host to over 700 Muslim guests, and followed it up with receiving a caravan of over 1000 Muslims from Futa Jallon. This was in 1859. In fact, the colonial officials were very indulgent towards Islam, led in this by the impressive Dr. Edward Blyden, perhaps the foremost black intellectual of the 19th century, and an acclaimed scholar of Arabic and Islam.

The Islam of the sword and empire, which governors, might prefer to promote existed alongside that form of Islam which was embraced by the ordinary person. And that form of the religion elicited an African response similar to the impact of revival religion. In the play there is constant mention of the Muslim creed, the *shahadah, la ilaha illa llahi,* that great monotheist affirmation which is also the assertion of the irreducible scriptural purity of Islam. What in fact happened to that formulation in Africa was that it was unscrambled and reconstituted as oral faith, a phrase of power which activates ancient oracles and is assimilated as a link in the chain by which the living and the dead are bound. Hardly the intention of pious Puritans of the plateau, but surely not less understandable for that.

The joining of the power of revival religion and the mystery of the Islamic *shahadah* with African religious values has created an indestructible tradition of a protean vitality. The African religious world is akindle with the unseen forces of another world. People pour libations not only in the brief, momentary flares of misfortune or death, but in the tension-filled business of everyday life and existence. And while they are about that they might also create elaborate aesthetic statements in art and ritual, both to circumvent the abrasiveness of direct challenge and to lock up in accessible form the otherwise unapproachable powers of the unseen. One of the great affirmations of ancient Africa is that Illness is not just a natural fact. It is a social event, and in its face society must intervene directly by ascertaining the cause and offering sacrifice to bring about healing. Witchcraft belongs to this social view of life. Society is concerned about the witch only when faced with a particular instance of bewitching. We might almost say, with some truth, that witches do not exist except when witchcraft has been proved. Consequently, witches have no social reality; only proven cases of *bewitching* might demand the prior existence of a witch as the agent of ill-will. Usually the witch is established from within the family or kin group, and it is rare to bring a witch in from outside the community. The empirical world of family quarrels, disagreements, grudges, spite and envy is the familiar pool into which the ingredients of a witch are discharged. Witches are not a separate social group of enemies but rather the state of broken relationship into which anyone may fall. Witchcraft is a crime only after genuine reconciliation with an estranged kin relative has failed utterly, and that is even without the sanction of permanent condemnation. No further doctrine is required to establish the existence of a witch than the social requirement to seek immediate redress in the circumstances of witchcraft.

Coming into such a world Islam was appropriately recast, with the Muslim cleric, known to us via the French sources as the *marabout*, now having to supply the amulets and other objects of protection against harm. Amulet making can be a lucrative enterprise although far more important is the power prestige it confers on the cleric. Many such clerics, parading the wares of piety, will make sure they allow a reputation for amulet-making to precede them into unfamiliar country. I am aware that such advance notification often opens the way for permanent settlement, but I am unsure about Islam emerging from that process completely unaffected.

It is this uncertainty, or something like it, that clings like static electricity to many of the characters of the play. In fact when they appear most certain about their precise religious identity, they seem most susceptible to the appeal of a different voice. Even Abass, that veteran representative of what in Freetown they used to call Johnny-Just-Come (JJC), even that travel-wise Abass is completely without recourse when finally confronted with the Juggernaut of revenge and counter-revenge. It is time to turn to the play itself as such.

The title of the play, *Worl' Do For Fraid,* is first mentioned by the character Pabuya, and that is not till Scene Three of Act One. By that time we have learnt a lot to make us ill at ease. Makalay, the wife of Chief Drissa, had died, and her distressed adopted daughter, who had survived her, had seen enough in dreams to make her feel time is out of joint. Her youth (she is only fifteen) makes an older woman, Nene, in her sixties, offer help and comfort. The truth of her disconsolation has to do with the murder of Makalay, for which Drissa is a prime suspect. Nene and Fatimah are the heroines of the play, the tragic figures whose world enfolds the disparate threads of a confused destiny. The action then shifts to the offering of a sacrifice at the grave of Makalay, and libation is poured.

In Scene Two of Act One, we are introduced to Baimbadi and his macabre preoccupation of imaginary grave-digging, at which point he is interrupted by Pastor Brown and his somewhat cavalier religious attitude. The good-natured altercation between the two hints enough at the depth of inter-religious harmony characteristic of much of West Africa. Eventually Pastor Brown, fortified with multiple religious identities, comes to the rescue of guilt-stricken Baimbadi and offers to lead him in a prayer for relief. Actually it turns out Pastor Brown cannot feign innocence, and is accessory to enough things to hang him thrice over. But religion, for what it is worth in these circumstances, covers him with a veil of modest dignity when the substance of virtue is in shreds. The multiple loyalties of a religious professional begin to tie him down like Gulliver and the tiny cords of numerous obligations that reduced him to utter helplessness. Pastor Brown's piety echoes with tones of a rehearsed creed, and that seems inadequate for people in desperate need of personal help. Fatimah then enters the stage, carrying a chicken for sacrifice, and is challenged by Saidu, her finance, who asserts that her intended sacrifice, now divulged before the world, would be ineffective. Scene Three of Act One brings us to Pabuya—a character of enormous significance, as I shall demonstrate in a moment. He sings in Temne, interspersed with popular songs of the period. He is bemoaning the passing of the good old days, more precisely, the twilight days of colonial rule when hope was high and spirits were free. His meditations on current political events are sharp, direct and prophetic. He turns the world upside down and reveals its inner workings with surgical incisiveness, although his clumsy, drunken manner could not be in grater contrast. He is indeed the precursor, the harbinger, of the Ghost of Makalay, who confronts Drissa with his horrible crime. We hear strains of *Hamlet* in the pursuing, castigating persistence of the Ghost. Murder had been committed under the innocent cover of matrimonial fidelity, and the shades will not be done yet.

Abass meets Drissa when the latter has been badly shaken and is diagnosed as having a mental breakdown by Abass, a psychiatrist by training. Drissa is to be committed to Kissy Mental Hospital, although Baimbadi, Abass's father, says Drissa has been bewitched and needs a different treatment. Before Drissa drifts off into the sunset of lunatic non-existence, Baimbadi blurts out the truth of their having conspired together to kill both Makalay and Abbi, her daughter, to secure chiefly office for Drissa. They had brought calamity upon themselves and the entire family. It transpires later that Fatimah herself had been violated in the process. At this point Abass is properly introduced to the family after returning from his training in England. He is tested for his fidelity to tradition, his former belief in dreams. Abass retorts to his inquisitors by affirming the values of hard work, rational thought and robust faith in the powers of human beings. By contrast, he argues, blacks are weighed down by the ponderous concerns of religion and obligations towards death. That, he contends, is the source of black disillusionment. Abass cannot help but be sucked into the world of Nene and Baimbadi. He asks Nene:

Nene, what is happening to Uncle Drissa? Why didn't you write about it? I look like a stranger in my own home. I have the feeling that something is knocking my heart almost to pieces.
    Softly, almost whispering.
What has happened to Fatimah? Why does she drag her feet as she walks? She is not sick, is she?

NENE
My son, we are all sick.
    Long pause.
The burdens of the past were too heavy; but the ones of the present are over-crushing. We may have to bear these burdens until the day we are buried.

ABASS

But life has to change. We can't go on this way. You are not as young as you used to be, and I am not either. We have to grow from the past.

NENE

Where will the change come from? We change our clothes every day. We want beautiful clothes, we wear caftans, we wear boubous, and big gowns, and we look different every minute. But do our minds match that beauty to which we pretend? That's the frightening thing, my son. Many things have changed but not for the better.

Nene admonishes Abass, "A child that crawls lives longer." To run in haste through the world is to risk falling into the holes with which the world is filled. The net is closing round Abass too. Nene recounts the story of an elephant turned beautiful woman to hunt the hunter that had been the scourge of animals like him. But before the hunter fell to her blandishments, his mother warned him about following the strange woman back into the far country. "Look closely under her ankles," the mother said. "Do her feet resemble those of a human being? Burn the gunpowder and you will find out." The smell of the powder chased off the elephant and the hunter was saved. Nene interprets the story for her son, Abass, so much at a disadvantage with his simple analytic mind. "Trust no one," she tells him. "No one. Talk a little and keep the rest to yourself." I should not think that was any more enlightening to Abass. A case of diminishing returns, I would have thought.

In Act Two, Scene Two, Abass defends his decision to return home and help in building the country. However, it would take a lot of defending in the face of wide spread corruption. But the challenge he hands down is turned away. Instead, Baimbadi and Pastor Brown, later joined by Joshua, invoke religious duty. The young men take over and are boastful of their powers. Brukus joins them, and engages in disrespectful parodying of Pastor Brown as primary school teacher. Brukus is a health inspector and gets his meat supply from deferential butchers in the local market. Abass calls it bribery in self-righteous indignation, but to Brukus and Joshua it is simple survival. Abass cuts in. "Joshua, our country is dying," and Joshua concurs with enthusiasm. Abass stirs the company with a report about a dream he had in London that he lost his back teeth, his molars, and that is interpreted as death in the family. Abass remains just as skeptical when Brukus tries to make him see that dreams carry meaning, or that ghosts do exist.

Act Two, Scene Three brings together the two central characters of Fatimah and Nene. A chicken is being sacrificed to avert disaster. Baimbadi is encountered and an enigmatic exchange takes place between him and Fatimah over a kola nut. Nene is left in the dark about the purpose of all that, though she is alert enough to be suspicious.

Act Three, Scene One brings in Pabuya, the market sweeper, too far down to worry about social or political reprisals, and yet close enough to diagnose with merciless clarity the sickness of society. It is ironic that a society on its way down may occasionally be lifted by the words of those at the bottom of the heap. Is that the contemporary African version of poetic justice? Pabuya describes the modern disdain for women who are preyed upon by unscrupulous young men, the parasites of Westernization. Then Fatimah's marriage to Saidu begins with the customary ceremony, but founders on the virgin test. Act Three, Scene Two shows Baimbadi licking his wounds for having failed to bring off the marriage of his daughter. He rails at Fatimah, "She is a slave" the breach with Fatimah is widened with Abass' intervention, and *p'ere et fils* are locked in bitter quarrel. Pastor Brown, with a penchant for colorful speech, butts in "When the tallest tree in the bush falls," he declares with oracular significance," all the little ones wither away." Then, victim to occupational hazard, he refers to Christ as symbol of universal suffering. Having burnt his bridges with his father, Abass turns to Pastor Brown with some sharp words about religion, which he says, "is mixed with tradition. Man's word becomes God's word—we are all mad, aren't we? Then I say God is dead!" he announces triumphantly. Those sentiments would have been shared by the Puritan reformers from the plateau, but they would have drawn a different conclusion. The rumble of the kettledrum heard at the beginning swells like death's messenger and we are left with carnage all over the stage. Not a shot is fired. Rather a veritable earthquake, as an act of God, flattens all, Fatimah, Drissa, and Baimbadi have all died.

In the third and final stage of my discussion, I should like to call attention to the theme of symbols in the play. First the kettledrum, the *tabule*. The drum consists of the wooden base on which the skin is mounted and pegged down on the sides. When it is struck it transmits a message which calls everyone within earshot. We might think of the wooden base as representing the stage, the skin as the script, and the drum-roll as the actors. The acoustic space is the world-view in which the message is received and appropriately interpreted. The events of the play cannot be conceived simply as cold facts of reality. The author is himself an actor, one who shapes his material to transmit a message. This is partly what I meant when I spoke about the social reality of life. The kettledrum vibrates with meaning long after it has been struck, and even when it stands still it resonates with meaning, for it represents also the world as a human construct. The dim, dolorous sounds played upon it are the death blows we deliver to our world. It stands outside our bodies but is in fact integral with our spirits. It is both the empirical trophy of our achievement and the symbolic organ of our inner being.

I must, in this connection, return to Pabuya. He is a market-sweeper. His place of work is a marvelous stage from which to view the world. And so he has acquired over the years an acute insight into human psychology. He has seen far too often the after-effects of human cupidity and the incessant haggling of the market-place. It is an unerring instrument for recording the pressures and moods of society. Then he gets drunk and enters into a state of semi-intoxication. His words, normally a departure from Standard English, now are infused with the heady impetuousness of a drunk. So he turns society upside down, reverses the norms and ascends his mount as the wise man of the age. He probes and exposes with loquacious appetite. His drunken state is itself a symbol of society in complete disarray, with the forces of disequilibrium in the ascendancy.

Out of the innumerable gaps opened by universal chaos, Pabuya arrives at what sane, sober people have missed or set their faces against. Seeing society from down under and now riding it in its upside-down condition, gives Pabuya an incomparable advantage. He shines from that intrinsic strength, the one bright spot in a land engulfed in darkness and death. His position is now at the boundary where the old and the new have met and produced tension. He therefore represents the significance of the 'threshold' for any future regeneration of society. A return to the past is clearly impossible. But equally disastrous is any unbridled charge into Westernization. Drissa as chief paid an unsustainable price for the privilege of traditional honor, and he obviously cannot be our guide. But Abass equally is less equipped to take us into the future, for it is doubtful if he, too, can survive only on a diet of incessant diatribe against tradition. In the end Pabuya must give us of his cutting humor so that we may be healed of crippling nostalgia and saved from a rapacious individualism.

Lamin Sanneh
Yale Divinity School

Lamin Sanneh is D. Willis James Professor of Missions and World Christianity, and Professor of History at Yale Divinity School.

A Note on the Play and Acknowledgments

Although this play and its sinister events are set in 1950, it is not simply a historical account: several ministers and high-ranking officers have committed such crimes against human dignity in the pursuit of power, fame, and position. Similar scenarios of ritual murder for political power may be traced back to the early 1930s, and such crimes are still committed behind the scenes. If we examine the political history of Sierra Leone, we are stunned and bewildered by events that shock the rational, civilized person. Sierra Leone is not the only theater where murder takes place on stage before the audience. But my intention as a writer is to dramatize this situation, telling the truth without any compromise. Let the play speak for the victims of such crimes wherever they may occur—*for murder, though it has no tongue, will speak with most miraculous organ.*

So much for the play. Now let me take this opportunity to thank a special group of people and individuals whose tremendous help and understanding made possible the writing and production of *Worl' Do For Fraid*. My special thanks and gratitude to Professor William Alfred of the English Department of Harvard, for helping in shaping, molding, and weaving the dramatic pattern of this play. Also to Professor Robert Chapman, for introducing a variety of Western playwrights and whose electrifying discussions of these authors helped to enrich my experience. Thanks to Mr. H.C. Mansfield, Jr., for introducing me to political thinkers of the West—Nietzsche, Hobbes, Heidegger, Machiavelli, etc. These authors' severe analyses of Man and Existence removed all doubts that Man is solely responsible for his own actions and must be held accountable for his success or failures. Thanks are due to Professor Martin Kilson, whose merciless and judicious criticism of Africa awakened in me a conscience of maturity for understanding the plight of the African in our time. Last but not least in this category is Professor Samuel H. Beer, for sharing his time and company with me in discussing politics, literature and sociology in reference to Africa.

The second category of people, whose tremendous support and help I received in the two productions of *Worl' Do for Fraid*, are as follows: Mr. James Spruill, who directed the staged reading of the play and the entire cast of the 1978 production. Special thanks to director David Montgomery for his enthusiastic support; to director Joe Manong and to Akosua Busia (who played Fatimah) for their ceaseless efforts in making the 1980 production a success. My special thanks and gratitude are due to the following who participated in the two symposia held at the Harvard Law School and the Harvard Science Center: Dr. Lawrence Kamara, Department of Sociology, University of Massachusetts; Professor Martha Nussbaum, Department of Philosophy, University of Chicago; Dr.

Bennet Simon, Harvard Medical School. Themes discussed were: (1) Witchcraft in Sierra Leone, (2) Conceptions of Good and Evil, (3) Dreams and Their African Interpretations, and (4) The Psychoanalytic Interpretation of Dreams.

Also, I would like to thank Professor David Levine and his wife Sarah for their interest in the play; President Matina S. Horner of Radcliffe College; Ms. Myra Mayman and Cathleen McCormack for their help in the 1984 production of the play at Agassiz House at Radcliffe; Professor Caldwell Titcomb of Brandeis University for his tremendous and enthusiastic support since the first production of the play, and for his taking time from his very busy schedule to transcribe the play's songs and to write the Afterword. Many thanks to all those who have been left out, but who, in my mind, share my experience and deserve my admiration and gratitude for all they did for me, especially my attorney and best friend Mr. Ian Shrank, his wife Lexa, and Dr. Lamin Sanneh, for his enlightening Introduction to the play.

> *Nabie Yayah Swaray*
> *Cambridge, Mass.*
> *May 17, 1986*

Original Casts of First Two Productions

Worl' Do For Fraid was first given a reading production by the Harvard Dudley House Drama Club and the New African Company at Lehman Hall, Harvard University, on April 22 and 23, 1978, with the following cast directed by Professor James Spruill of Boston University:

NENE	Janet Young
FATIMAH	Francine Mills
BAIMBADI	James Spruill
PASTOR BROWN	Vernon Blackman
CHIEF DRISSA	Jay Foote
GHOST OF MAKALAY	Gwen Mason
PABUYA	Nabie Yayah Swaray
POLICEMAN	Paul Everet
ABASS	Edward Montero
JOSUAH	Paul Everet
BRUKUS, SAIDU	Marlon Riggs
STAGE MANAGER	Betty McNally
MUSICIANS	Val Parker, Henry Cobb

In 1980 it was produced in a revised version at The Boston Arts Groups Theatre, in Boston, with the following cast directed by Joe Manong:

NENE	Deborah Adams
FATIMAH	Akosua Busia
BAIMBADI	Eddie Cabral
PASTOR BROWN	Jerry Bangs
CHIEF DRISSA	Fredric Hayes
GHOST OF MAKALAY	Brenda Ryans
PABUYA	Nabie Yayah Swaray
POLICEMAN	Thomas Jeffrey Giles
SAIDU	Marshall Singletary Maxwell
ABASS	Emeka Kalu Ezera
JOSUAH	Andrew McAchern
BRUKUS	Richard Mizell
DANCERS	Nneka Dike, Pauline Venzen
GODMAMY	Doyin Ashamu
PRODUCERS	Louise Edoze, Emeka Dike
SET DESIGNER	Joe Manong
COSTUMES	Doyin Ashamu
TECH DIRECTOR	Bert de Pass
FLUTE	Salim Michel Washington
DRUMS	Olof Olson

Act One

Well, heaven forgive him, and forgive us all.
Some rise by sin, and some by virtue fall:
Some run from breaks of ice, and answer none,
And some condemned for a fault alone.

— William Shakespeare, *Measure for Measure*

Cast

DRISSA, Chief of Kissy Mess-Mess Village

BAIMBADI, twin brother of Drissa

ABASS, second son of Baimbadi

SAIDU, first son of Baimbadi

PASTOR BROWN, friend of the Bangura family

JOSHUA and BRUKUS, schoolmates of Abass and friends of the family

PABUYA, market sweeper

POLICEMAN

GHOST OF MAKALAY, wife of Drissa and twin sister of Nene

NENE, wife of Baimbadi and mother of Saidu and Abass

FATIMAH, adopted daughter of Makalay and Saidu's bride-to-be

GODMAMY, observer of wedding ceremonies

DANCERS, male and female

Scene One

TIME
July, 1950: the rainy season.

PLACE
Kissy Mess-Mess, a village on the edge of Freetown, Sierra Leone.

SETTING
Chief Drissa's house and compound. The chief's house, made of concrete blocks with a corrugated iron roof, is flanked to the left by Nene's adobe hut and to the right by the young men's bungalow, also of concrete construction; both are attached to the main house. A gigantic flamboyant tree towers over the main house; its huge, spreading branches, thick with dark purple flowers, cover the entire roof. There are three doors: stage left, a narrow door leads to the village cemetery; between the bungalow and the main house, an arched gateway leads into the backyard; at stage right is another door that leads out to a country road. Before the house is a spacious compound that occupies all of center stage. It is a gathering place for tribal meetings and for the discussion of family matters and town problems. Center stage left is a tabule¹ drum which hangs on a branching stick. The stage is in darkness; only the harsh and glowing radiance of the flamboyant flowers lights the roof of the house. Loud thunder, lightning, and the cries of an owl and an engbonke² bird break the deep and still silence of this night. As the storm dies down, a melody is played on a bamboo flute offstage; it tells of bad dreams. The shrill voices of the dead blend with the sound of the

---

¹ **Tabule.** A drum that announces death, or the arrival of a chief or a village celebrity.
² **Engbonke.** A bird associated with witchcraft. Its cries are an ill omen.

flute. Their confused rhythm is drowned by the sound of the tab-ule, which is beaten violently—three hesitating beats that signify a death. The curtain rises. Before us is a small room: NENE'S hut. The stage is still dark. Brutal, frightening voices are heard offstage. FATIMAH, the adopted daughter of MAKALAY, is lying on a straw mat, tormented by bad dreams. She is only fifteen. Nene, a woman in her later sixties, is standing behind Fatimah, bowed and bewildered by her niece's strange behavior and the unnatural hap-penings of the night. She is in grief at the strange death of her twin sister Makalay, wife of CHIEF DIRSSA, and at the strange disap-pearance of her niece ABBI, the daughter of Drissa and Makalay. As the light rises Fatimah, panic-stricken, jumps up, confused and emotionally broken; screams and hides behind Nene.

    FATIMAH
    In fear and desperation.
Auntie! Auntie! Auntie, they've come for me!
    Long pause.

    NENE
    Concealing her shock.
What is this, my child? What is behind this strange behavior?
Fatu? Look at me in the face. What is the matter?

    FATIMAH
    Nene forces her to sit on the mat. After a long pause.
    Weakening.
Auntie, I...I am finished
    Pause. Nene kneels before her, frightened, but with much
    sympathy and affection.

NENE

What? What do you mean, Fatimah?

FATIMAH
Still weeping and frightened.
They have taken away my life—

NENE
Smiles skeptically. Concerned, she speaks severely to Fatimah, almost pleading.
You will not do this to us, Fatimah, will you?

FATIMAH
Pauses thoughtfully, then speaks abruptly.
They came for me and took away my life.
Nene, wide-eyed, mouth open, perplexed. Fatimah shows her the palm of her hands.
See! I can't open my eyes. I'm now empty like a mortar...
Weeps.
Just a wooden gong—there's nothing left in me, nothing!
In a broken voice.
Can't you understand? Oh, auntie, I'm finished.
Nene stares deeply into her eyes as Fatimah gains control of herself and says forcefully,
My life was skinned away from my guts.
Pause.
I fought with all my strength, but I was overpowered—defeated and paralyzed. I...watched them running away with it. I cried, "Give it back to me! Give it back to me!"
Pointing to an imaginary cotton tree.
There! There it hangs, on their bewitched cotton tree; drip-

ping with blood.

> *Pause.*

I'm slowly withering like a creeping plant burnt out by the sun.

> *Pause.*

My end will soon come when my life which they took away from me stops dripping with blood.

> *Nene is frozen in deep thought. After a brief silence, Fatimah slowly begins to rise. Covers her face with her hands and like a cow stung by a gadfly screams and points to a framed picture of Makalay, hanging on the wall.*

There! There! That's her, Auntie!

NENE
> *Rising, she observes Fatimah with mixed feelings. (It is a sin against the dead to expose their pictures, especially if the bereaved family is still in mourning.) She goes and turns the picture against the wall. Returns to Fatimah.*

It is not my sister's picture that is the cause of your acting so strangely.

FATIMAH
> *Now sitting still beside Nene.*

No, Auntie. I—I dreamed—oh Auntie—
> *Breaks off again.*

NENE
> *Holding Fatima's hand.*

Now be quiet and tell me what you saw.

FATIMAH
With her head bowed.
...In that dream, I saw a pregnant woman with a sword through her. Her entrails were dripping with blood. She—she held in her arms half of a child badly mutilated... I only saw half of this child; it was a bloody child. Then walking behind her was a young girl about my height. She too was bleeding and crying: "Give me my heart." Then I saw her pointing towards the compound, and before they vanished, the woman carrying the mutilated half-child spat on the chair of Chief Drissa, and the whole compound was flooded with human blood... Oh, Auntie... what good will this bring to us?
Screams.

NENE
Restraining her?
Now sit here. Do you hear me?
With a deep sigh.
God Almighty! Fatimah, no one will destroy—

FATIMAH
Sobbing.
Can't you understand? I'm finished. I'm ruined for life.
Pause.

NENE
Angrily and yet with much sympathy.
No one is after you—no one. If you have killed a lucky snake that bears cowries on its head[3]... Then you've brought de-

---

[3] **A lucky snake that bears cowries on its head.** Several kinds of snake are so marked and may bring good or bad fortune, depending on the species.

struction to yourself. Sit here! I have long been trying to find a convenient time to speak to you—No, this isn't the right time either. But... but I have to do it now before we all drown in the flood you dreamed tonight. I won't allow this behavior to continue any longer. Listen! This is not the way you used to behave. I'm not the only one that has noticed your odd and unusual actions. Some good neighbors of mine have repeatedly warned me to keep a keen eye on you—

FATIMAH
Angrily and in tears.
So they have been spying—they destroyed my life. Liars! Hypocrites! These nasty people—

NENE
Now be still. Listen to me, you stubborn child. I noticed this queer behavior of yours after the Forty-Day Ceremony of my late sister, Makalay.
To herself.
God have mercy on her soul.

FATIMAH
Tightly.
And on me, too!

NENE
With a troubled smile, and severely, to Fatimah.
Nowadays you keep away from people. You stare piercingly at things and people, and fix your eyes at invisible objects. Sometimes you beat your breasts like an uninitiated girl afraid

of the Bondo drums[4]...

Fatima stirs.

Yes, don't deny that. Some say you sometimes stand at a place hours on end talking to invisible things. No, I've not finished yet! Some say you bite your fingers, pull your tongue like a snake, stamp your foot harshly on the ground, and make all kinds of grimaces at people. They say you clap your hands, dance, and sing songs of the dead. Again, I will not help you kill your lucky snake that bears cowries on its head lest it bring destruction to our family. Have you killed one? Answer me!

FATIMAH
In a broken voice.
Auntie, I did not.

Quickly and in tears.

I was the snake that was killed. I did not bring destruction to this family. It's I who am destroyed—I'm finished... They have my life hanging on their bewitched cotton tree, and every day they suck my blood.

Showing her hands.

Don't you see how pale I am! No, you can't help me... You can't, and you won't—

NENE
Rises, takes off her head tie and ties it around her waist; angrily shaking her finger at Fatimah.
What! You, a seedling, a yam tendril, a baby still crying for its mother's back... Who else will help you? Tell me, if I can't,

---

[2] **Bondo drums.** Used in the initiation rites of young girls, which are conducted by the women's Bondo Society.

who else will?—huh? You with your dreams.

> *Returning to her bed, sits. The flute begins to play off-stage and the lights are now bright and steady.*

Now listen, perhaps you don't know how you came to be a member of this family.

FATIMAH
Embracing Nene.
Auntie, now I will behave. Please, believe in me.

NENE
Sighing deeply, holding Fatimah's hands.
Oh, my child... sometimes I thought it was wise to conceal the facts from you. But it won't be of any help now. We must be free and open with one another. I call you my child, my daughter, and so did my late sister, Makalay.

> *In a broken voice.*

What I have to say may seem to you like the dream you've just had.

> *Drops her head.*

Makalay...was...not...your mother. But that's not what I want to say to you now.

> *Wipes her tears.*

FATIMAH
Also in tears.
Oh, Auntie, you're crying. Please, please, don't...

NENE
Now composed.
You don't know who your mother was, and you will never

see her like again. She was a woman strong, beautiful, and loving...Mamusu was her name—

Fatimah bursts into tears.

Now listen, my child. Your mother was my best and only friend at Kawula. We were born on the same day, so we were told. But a strange thing happened.

Wringing her hands.

I can still remember that horrible night, how she suffered on her deathbed. God have mercy on us.

Breaks off, now weeping.

FATIMAH
Kneeling before Nene.

Auntie, please, please don't cry. God will have mercy on us.

Short pause.

NENE

Before your mother died, Makalay and I were in the room where she was laid out. Makalay and others were struggling to keep you alive; you never cried, and they had to beat pans and drums to make you cry. I stayed and sat by your mother. Before she died, when we had given up all hope, she held my hands and pressed them in hers. With a dying voice, she called my name three times: "Nene, Nene, Nene" Everyone was crying. And then she whispered to me, with my hands still in hers. "Nene," she said, "It was God's Providence that I should leave behind me my own seed... It was ordained by god that the child had to be born by me... I'm dying, but if the baby lives, let it be yours forever. She belongs to you and your sister."

In a broken voice.

And then she died.

Fatimah is now crying.

My child, her last words were like words that came from the God Almighty. It was then that I made this promise: to treat you just as I treat my own children.

Rising.

I would rather die than break that promise. No! You can't do this to me, Fatimah. You must be open to me. I will do everything to help you.

FATIMAH

Auntie, I have no other mother except you. The one who I thought was my mother is dead. My real mother I never saw. I opened my eyes and saw you, and until now, I never knew who was my mother...

NENE

So you must not hide anything from me.

FATIMAH

Her whole body trembling.

Oh, Auntie, I promise—the dream, the dream—I heard voices and then a voice kept saying to me, "You must speak what you saw. You must speak what they did to you. Speak! Speak!"

NENE

In a subdued voice, but very courageously.

Fatimah, I will try to help you just as I did in the case of your mother. You are young and strong...

FATIMAH
Oh, my mother, oh Mamusu; where is she now, oh God help her, help me!

NENE
No, don't think this way. I'm the only one who can help you. But you must be willing to help yourself. Today is Saturday. And my sister's death was brought home to us on a Saturday. Makalay's death still remains a mystery to us, and her daughter's death too. It's still dark but I must perform the sacrifice at my sister's grave tonight.
  Pointing to a tied hen and a bottle of palm wine.
You will come with me to the cemetery. We must offer this sacrifice before dawn. My son, Abass, comes home today. For ten years he has been away in strange countries—in the land of white people, they say. How will I receive him? Will my dead sister forgive me if I should dance to welcome my son? What will our neighbors say? I know they will murmur with dissatisfaction and whisper, "How easily we forget those that were part of our world." I know it. I know they will. If it weren't for that crazy Baimbadi who, like a cockerel, is trumpeting to the whole world about my son's arrival... Also, you know that Drissa is no longer the chief of this town; poor man, they took his staff[5] from him. Because of this, he's almost losing his senses. He carries his own load on his head. Drissa cannot come with me to his wife's grave to offer this sacrifice... It's you whom I will depend on.
  Nene goes to where the sukublai[6] sits and takes out an old

---

[5] **Staff**. A special gold-headed walking stick, the symbol of chiefly authority.
[6] **Sukublai**. A straw basket.

fashioned gown.

Here, wear this. This was our mother's gown. With this, nothing will happen to you.

      Helps Fatimah wear the gown.

FATIMAH
With renewed confidence.

Now I feel safe.

      Nene slowly opens the door. It's still dark. Fatimah follows behind.

NENE

Don't forget the lambe.

FATIMAH

What is it?

NENE

What! Don't you know what a lambe is?—The libation. Perhaps you are not in the proper frame of mind. Take the palm wine bottle and bring it with you... It's still dark out here.

FATIMAH
Quickly

Oh yes—the libation.

      Picks up the palm wine bottle and returns to the doorway.

NENE

Can you see the stars?

FATIMAH

No! No! Auntie, the stars have disappeared. The clouds are still dark.

Both are standing in the doorway.

NENE

You can't even see the hair in your skin, can you?

FATIMAH

Trembling.

No, Auntie. There! There!

NENE

Interested.

What is it?

FATIMAH

Oh, no. I thought it was a fixed star.

NENE

Disappointed.

A fixed star?

FATIMAH

No, I only saw shooting stars, falling from one end to the other...

NENE

Impatient.

We must not stand here. Come! We must do this sacrifice before dawn. I also have to prepare for my son's arrival.

15

FATIMAH
Mutters as they leave stage left.
If only the night could see and speak, daylight would weep...
She abruptly starts.

NENE
What!

FATIMAH
I thought I heard the cockcrowing.

BLACK OUT

Scene Two

The rain has ceased, but there are still snatches of thunder and lightning. Then a woman and a young girl are heard wailing off-stage. The wailing voices are accompanied by the beat of a tabule. This confused sound continues. As the light comes on, BAIMBA-DI, dressed in his dark velvet pajamas (a gift from his educated son, ABASS), is seen sitting quietly, lost in deep thought and in grief. He seems to be talking to himself, or addressing an imaginary person on stage, but we hardly hear the words. He smiles from time to time—a bewildered smile. The tabule is beaten again—three hesitating beats that remind us of death or a house in mourning. Baimbadi, now in his late seventies, seems to be a lively man. But as this scene opens, his joy at the homecoming of an educated son is clouded by fear. He advances towards center stage, arms clapped behind his back, as the noise begins to fade away.

> BAIMBADI
> *Lost in deep thought.*

What a frightening night.

> *Three hesitating beats of a tabule are heard offstage. He is transfixed. As the crescendo mounts, frightening him, the light glares harshly on his face. He begins to moan and becomes excited; then paces off an imaginary grave.*

Twelve feet long.

> *Pause.*

Six feet deep.

> *He sweats profusely as he digs with imaginary pick and shove, finishing the first grave. Then he stands exhausted with his arms akimbo; sighs deeply and groans.*

Six feet deep... That's it! This can hide a vulture, a witch bird, a wolf, a... kriffi.[7]

> *Pause. Paces off the second grave and digs it. Troubled, he wipes his face and digs the third grave. After completing it.*

Yes, sir! That is it! That's it! Six feet under...

> *Thinks, then sighs deeply, shrugging off the thought.*

No! No! It cannot be now. Not today! Don't you remember?

> *Pauses.*

My son is coming home today.

> *The light fades on him. He is left in the darkness. Then as the light comes on, PASTOR BROWN, a Lutheran priest and friend of Baimbadi, is heard whistling offstage. He is in his late sixties, full of energy—a religious fanatic. He enters stage left. He is dressed up in a black gabardine suit; holds his hat cocked against his shoulder, and carries a walking stick and a Bible. As he advances towards Baimbadi, his whistling grows louder and louder. Baimbadi is seriously disturbed, being a Muslim.*

BAIMBADI

> *Awakening from his lethargy and hallucinations, briskly walks towards Pastor Brown, silencing him.*

Pastor!

PASTOR BROWN

> *Delighted. Takes off his hat, holds it high in the air and with fanatic enthusiasm shouts.*

The Lord be praised! Hallelujah!

> *Continues to whistle as he moves towards Baimbadi.*

The Lord be praised—

---

[7] **kriffi.** A kind of spirit, either good or bad.

BAIMBADI
Disturbed by the strange behavior of Pastor Brown.
Pastor! Pastor! It's not quite morning.
With some difficulty.
I... don't expect a man of your age to whistle like a child.
Besides, you are a religious man. A religious man must not
whistle. You know very well that whistling is against the Is-
lamic faith. In a strictly Islamic home, whistling is the devil's
work. Peaceful angels will never set their feet on a place where
men whistle, and whistle. Such a home belongs to Satan.

PASTOR BROWN
Almost laughs at the idea; then defensively,
Oh, Baimba, you Muslims have a queer way of praising God.
What! Must I not whistle and praise the Lord God Almighty?
I was whistling a religious hymn. Besides, today is the finest
day God has ever sent to us. The sun is shining. The storm
has died down; the clouds have disappeared. You can see the
green valley and the beautiful flamboyant flowers.
Seeing the troubled face of his friend.
Why? Are you not well? What is the matter with you? Abass,
your only educated son, is coming home today. That's why I
am here; to welcome him home. What else can a man ask of
God? You Muslims expect much from God. You should be
happy and praise the Lord for such good fortune. How many
homes or towns or districts that can boast of having a doctor?
This is the only home in this town with a doctor. Fall on your
knees and praise the Lord.

BAIMBADI
Subdued.

19

How should I praise him?
>*After a pause.*

I... I was... digging—

PASTOR BROWN
>*Not understanding him.*

Yes, a man must dig and turn the dust over and over if one is to find the meaning of life. What were you digging?

BAIMBADI
>*Trembling, and wringing his hands. Softly and in a subdued voice.*

Graves.

PASTOR BROWN
>*Shocked.*

Graves! For whom?
>*Long pause. Then turns to Baimbadi, who is bowed by guilt.*

Baimba! Graves for whom? What! So early in the morning?

BAIMBADI
>*Turns sullenly to Pastor Brown; almost at his mercy.*

Pastor. I'm... caught in a trap.
>*Pause.*

I can't face God. Allah sees everything. I'm afraid—

PASTOR BROWN
>*Seizing the opportunity to preach to his friend.*

Caught in a trap? Oh, Baimba, you are not a rat. You are a man of God. You must not allow things that frighten children to bother you. You know, I came by the church and I was delighted to hear the strong voices of the young children so early in the morning. I thought the heavy rain would keep them at home. But the church was full—young, old, beggars, cripple—all praying to the Lord. And you know what? I was touched by the song.

>*Sings.*

You going to reap whatever you sow
You going to reap whatever you sow
Down by the river, way up in the mountain
You going to reap whatever you sow

>*Falls on his knees, Bible in hand.*

Oh, Baimba, I was deeply touched. No, Baimba, the young are not lost yet. God is not dead yet. God is not dead yet.

>*Rises.*

This world will wake up to His call again; and young and old will sing and stand before Him like saints, and they will be forgiven like Christians.

>*Looks piercingly at Baimba.*

Now, Baimba, kneel with me. Kneel with me.

>*He forces him to kneel in prayer with him. Holds his hat up to towards the heavens. Prays with religious ecstasy. Baimba does not utter a word. He is benumbed and guilt-laden.*

Oh Lord, oh Lord, oh Omnipotent Lord. God Almighty, let the dews of heaven visit my heart. Bring prosperity to those in need. Restore faith to those that have fallen on thorny ground. Bring light where there is darkness; forever and forever. Amen. Say "amen," Baimba.

BAIMBADI
Tightly, almost tongue-tied.

Amen.

Pause.

But Pastor, Nene, my wife, is deeply troubled by her sister's death. Drissa is no longer himself. How will I face God?

Pause.

How should I explain these things to my son, Abass? These things that are happening to our family...

After a long pause.

Two months have passed since Drissa became Chief of Kissy Mess-Mess... and it was a night like this that the elders decided to take Chief Drissa to the sacred bush. You remember?

PASTOR BROWN
Faintly.

I remember.

BAIMBADI
He is beginning to feel like himself again.

The kabap[8] bird sat on the rooftop and with shrill cries sang for days on end. And now Drissa is running round in the town—losing his wits. Makalay is dead. Her daughter is dead too. Fatimah is behaving strangely.

Pause.

And today my son, Abass, comes home. I never mentioned in my letters these things that are happening to our family. How will I face my son?

---

[8] **Kabap.** A bird whose cries foretell and express important life event, e.g., illness and death. Its cries are interpreted by old people who have developed this skill.

Pauses. Now almost in tears.

Children always ask questions... What answer will I give him?

Pastor Brown tries to comfort him. Weeps in the arms of Pastor Brown.

Oh, Pastor, our house is ruined. I'm... I'm ashamed. I cannot face him.

PASTOR BROWN

With much confidence.

Baimbadi! You are the father in this house, not Abass. Besides, Abass will not be much interested in things like this, you'll see. It is you who have to believe in God. It is not your part to question God's work. Do you remember Job? The Book of Job! Job in the Old Testament? You have heard me preach on the Book of Job. Who will explain why pregnant women die in childbirth? Who will explain why innocent children die? Who will explain why this one is poor and that one is rich? God gives and takes away: all is God's work. Do you think the rain falls only on one man's roof? Fortune and misfortune are man's closest neighbors. Why do Muslims say first, "Subhana Lai, Subhana Lai": God is mysterious. Then "Alahu-akbar, Alahu-akbar": God is great. Then finally. "Al hamdu Lilah, Al hamdu Liilah": that is, I thank God. Now go in and get dressed.

Baimbadi is deeply touched and consoled, his faith renewed.

Baimbadi! Do you hear me?

BAIMBADI

He rises to go, slowly takes Pastor Brown's hand. They embrace with joy.

23

Pastor, you are the only friend I've got. Now that Drissa is sick, I'm the only one left to look after the family.

PASTOR BROWN
Releasing Baimba.
Love God! With God, all things are possible.

BAIMBADI
As he turns to go.
Yes, Allah is great. I believe in that.

PASTOR BROWN
A horn sounds offstage.
Ah! There is the boat! Just arriving. Remember, Baimba, God will not leave His children in the darkness forever.
After a long thought, quotes.
"He that troubleth his own house shall inherit the wind."
Breathes with relief.
God help us!

BAIMBADI
Returns. Well dressed in his white gown, white shoes and cap.
Pastor, how do I look?

PASTOR BROWN
Excellent! Excellent! You look like Father Abraham.
Pause.
On a fine day like this, and a son coming home. You must be proud of yourself.
Seeing a letter in his hand.

What's that?

> BAIMBADI

This was his last letter he wrote me. Here, read it.
> *Hands the letter to Pastor Brown.*

Have it.

> PASTOR BROWN
> *Delighted that he himself can read and write.*

Oh, he asks if all is well and whether the family is quite well.
> *Strains his eyes to read a strange word, perhaps new to him. Puts on his glasses.*

Hmmmm!

> BAIMBADI

What's that?

> PASTOR BROWN
> *Embarrassed.*

These young men of today write in strange words. You see, the Apostles spoke in different tongues when the Holy Spirit descended upon them. Hmmm! Hmm! Hmmm—
> *Turns the letter over and over. Wipes his glasses. Stares piercingly at the letter. Baimbadi, arms akimbo, is both proud and surprised that his son could write such a difficult letter. Pastor Brown is shocked that he cannot read it, and struggles with it.*

Idio...idio—
> *Angered.*

Idio—what?
> *Slaps his forehead.*

Idio... Idiosyncra...

Pause.

Good heavens! I can't understand it!

Baimbadi laughs. Then BLACK OUT.

As the light comes up again, Fatimah is seen standing at center stage. She is dressed in her sacrificial gown of red, white, and black, and carries a live chicken in her hands. As she begins to move towards the house SAIDU, her husband to be, enters stage left, dressed in wide khaki trousers and a large, flowing white shirt that reaches below the waist; shaved head and bare feet. He is shocked at seeing Fatimah so early in the morning and walks briskly towards her.

SAIDU

In a threatening tone of voice.

Stop there!

Fatimah keeps trembling with the chicken in her hands. Saidu pulls her by the ear. Almost impatient with her.

Can't you talk! Huh? Can't you talk? So this is what you've been doing. The night is your friend. During the day you turn dumb, but not at night. Where have you been all night?

Fatimah does not answer. She keeps digging the ground with her right foot.

Is this what you do when you are asked? What are you doing with that chicken in your hands? I know you are trying to sacrifice that deathly chicken to your kriffis to make us tongue-tied while you get away with your crimes. No! Big Sisi![9]

Fatimah opens her mouth.

---

[9] **Sisi.** A grown woman who sexually pursues very young men.

You stand there with your mouth open? Your kriffis have failed you. As long as I have seen that chicken, your sacrifice is spoiled. Our wedding is only three weeks away, and as soon as Abass settles down, we will fix the day for the wedding ceremony. I won't waste any time with you. You never expected me to be here, did you?

> *Saidu starts. Fatimah murmurs. Saidu stops and turns sullenly to her.*

Are you denying that you didn't sleep in that mud hut last night with Nene? I know why you are so bold these days. You were never brought up here like an adopted child. Uncle Drissa and Baimbadi love you so much that you can't even love other people. They never taught you how to love other people...not even how to love your future husband—am I wrong? You will not deny that, will you?

> *Breathlessly.*

You are my adopted wife; you know it. Uncle Drissa and Baimbadi will never be a husband to you. They are your foster fathers, and by right I am your future husband.

> *Almost shouting.*

I will not blame you! It is the fault of Uncle Drissa and Baimbadi—they have Spoiled you! You are nothing but a spoiled child. Take that chicken away!

> *Saidu angrily exits stage right. Fatimah is left on stage, transfixed and transmuted; then in a fiery outburst, shouts.*

FATIMAH
SPOILED!

BLACK OUT

Scene Three

On the same day. Before us is an open market, it is now morning. As the stage light comes alive, a wooden table, almost falling apart, is seen backstage. In the corner behind the table is a heap of decaying filth and empty garbage tins. A tabule is beaten viciously, then three hesitating beats. The light dies with the fading beat of the tabule. Then a flute is played off-stage rapid, yet somber and pathetic. As the light begins to glow upon the table, CHIEF DRISSA is seen standing center stage, bowed by grief. He walks quietly with his arms behind his back. He wears a woman's big red frock, is barefoot, and carries a stick, he does not put down. He is transfixed; with disgust shrugs off the word, "masamafu."[10] Repeats, "masamafu." He quietly disappears and settles behind the table. PABUYA appears stage right. He is a thin, lanky man, about fifty. He wears a long, ragged white shirt; carries a bottle of water, a bundle of whips, and a broom. He enters the market walking backwards. Sings heartily.

> PABUYA
> *With all his might.*
Maienkayray! Maienkayray![11]
Eeyaw k'thuma
K'thuma, k'thuma, k'thuma, k'thuma, kere day keet!
"Asana!"
"Na!"
aw-way me ba k'ruhm to woor-ay!
Bomsowkaw,aw po mee ketha

---

[10] **Masamafu.** Drissa's pronunciation of "je m'enfous": I don't care.

[11] **Maienkayray...** The translations of this and the other songs will be found with the musical transcriptions at the end of the play.

Ee yaw, "Woyo, Woyo, Maienkayray.

> *Dances and continues to sing as he advances toward center stage.*

Ee sawthaw tha-naw uhngyeek thawn-pay.
Kere day keet. Ee vowye
Ee bawthayresaw, kere day keet.

> *Long pause; then softly sings.*

Ee yaw, woyo, woyo! Ng na gbothawng, kuh foyay,
Pa gbothawng, kuh condemn!
Ee yaw, woyo, woyo, wo-yo!
Ee yaw,woyo, woyo, Maienkay-ray!

> *Laughs loudly and long. Puts down the bottle. Beats himself happily across the chest and forehead, pleased with himself. He studies the marketplace closely, and then takes the bottle out of his pocket. Performs a quick ritual ceremony to drive evil sprits and bad luck from the market before it opens: he goes to an imaginary door, stage right, opens the bottle, puts some water in his mouth, gargles, and spits on the doorway; then takes his whip and begins to whip imaginary spirits in the air.*

All bad people for go!
All bad people for go!
All evil spirit for go!
All bad sababu,[12] for go!
Only good people for stay near this market.

> *Repeats the same ceremony at the other two imaginary doors. Returns to center stage and does the same, then begins to sweep. A flute is played to the tune of "Fire, fire, fire, ma, fire dey come." He bursts out laughing and*

---

[12] **Sababu.** Luck: It could be good luck or bad luck; it depends on the outcome of the circumstances.

picks up the song, singing.

Fire, fire, fire mama,
Fire dey cam.
Fire, fire, fire mama,
Fire, dey cam.
I want to see my loving wife,
Loving wife I love so well.
Fire, fire, fire baby-yoh!
Fire dey cam.

Long pause. Then begins to sing again.

Wherever I go,
Sweetie palm wine dey wait for me.
I board a bus to Lum'ly,
I met a bus conductor,
Five shillings he charged me
For sak' of my education.
Boys and girls were laughing,
They say I was a drunkard,
But I am a free-born,
And Freetown is my colony!
Everywhere I go,
Sweetie palm wine dey wait for me.
Everywhere I go,
Sweetie palm wine dey wait for me.

The flute continues to play, to the tune of "Wherever I go."

Pabuya stops. Recalls the good old days.

Oh, them days!

Laughs and slaps his forehead.

Them good old days them sweet like Kingimy bonga.[13]

Shakes his head.

But them days tiday sour like sour-sour.[14] Ah. Yoni boy![15]
Tiday push done com per shurb. Tiday na so so trouble.[16]

*Laughs and continues to sweep in style. Stops; addresses
an object or an imaginary person.*

Oh yes-sir! Na trouble make monkey eat pepper. Everywhere
you go, na wahala! Up Country, na wahala! You go Freetown, na wahala.[17]

Pause.

Peace nor go be wusai sense nor day.[18]

Goes closer to the audience; almost whispering.

Then old days, you go be chief if you nor get chief blood?

Pause.

You mus'ge' chief blood! 'Cause you nor get chief blood,
kriffis go kill you if you nor get chief blood. You sleep na
sacred bush, them kriffis go kill you. But today all man wan'
be chief. Na so ay be oh! Tiday, all three en' ten pence. Sour
cream en ogiri all na the same pot.[19]

Laughs. Sweeps, stops, a little thoughtful.

---

[13] **Kingimy bonga.** Fish (bonga) from the Kingimy market in Freetown.
(The g in Kingimy is pronounced as is general).

[14] **Sour-sour.** A seasoning.

[15] **Yoni boy.** A boy from the village of Yoni.

[16] **Tiday push…na so trouble.** "Today, push has come to shove. Today
there's a lot of trouble."

[17] **Na trouble…na wahala."** Only great hunger compels a monkey to eat pep-
pers. Everywhere you go, there's trouble. In the countryside, trouble!
You go to Freetown, there's trouble."

[18] **Peace nor go be wusai sense nor day.** "Peace can't exist where people
lack sense."

[19] **Na so ay be oh… na the same pot.** "That's just how it is. Today they're
all the same: sour cream and ogiri seasoning, all in the same pot."

Jus' see dat chief of Kissy Mess-Mess, Pa Drissa. Dat man nor get chief blood. E buy him crown. Now the kriffis go drive him crazy.

> *Shrugs his shoulders and strikes his hand in disbelief.*

Dis pa Drissa go die like yuba.[20] Go die for corruption!

> *Laughs. Drissa stirs from his corner and Pabuya sees him.*

Who are you?

> *Drissa does not answer. Drissa rises. Pabuya in fright.*

You nor ge'ess?

> *Dirssa gives him a troubled smile. Pabuya is confused, does not know whether to stay or run. As Drissa begins to move towards him, Pabuya jumps in confusion, almost flees; then turns to him.*

You nor answer me! You go answer master. You go answer to Chief Drissa na Lock-up. Me go call police, now, now, now.

> *Runs offstage. Drissa rises, holding pieces of paper. He puts the papers on the floor and sets them on fire. As the newspapers blaze, a wild gust of wind sweeps across the stage, and the fire is covered by a mass of thick smoke. THE GHOST OF MAKALAY appears from the smoke. She is tall and shrouded with a bloodstained white sheet. Drissa jumps as the ghost advances towards him. The stage lights now turn blue.*

DRISSA
Quietly.

I lit the papers to warm myself. Where is the fire?

> *Retreating and addressing the ashes while the ghost stands still.*

---

[20] **Yuba.** Vulture.

Where is the fire? I say come back to life!

> *Seeing the ghost.*

Who are you? Now go away!

> *Attempts to strike the ghost but is overpowered; helpless,
> he kneels at a distance from the ghost. Now in a subdued
> voice.*

Please don't... I'm cold... cold like the ashes there.

GHOST

Drissa, I am the ghost of your wife, Makalay.

DRISSA

Trembling feverishly.

Makalay?—my wife! Didn't we bury you with all rites due to
the dead? Why have you come again to torment me?

GHOST

Still with a calm voice.

Drissa, I was once your wife. How did I annoy you? How did
I displease you? How did I offend you?

DRISSA

Covering his eyes, panic-stricken.

Makalay! I can see, I can see.

GHOST

You never had eyes to see. But I have come to tell you that
you and your family stand on the edge of misery.

DRISSA

In a tearful tone.

What have I done to you?

GHOST

I was to live seventy years on earth, but you cut my life off and sent me to my grave before my time.

DRISSA
Still on his knees.

Oh God.

GHOST
Earnestly.

You will hear everything. I will tell it all.

DRISSA

Well, then—

GHOST

All is not well for you, Drissa. What benefit did you get in my death? Answer me!
Drissa screams and covers his face.

We have husbands to give us their last blessings before we are laid in our graves. But yours were human sacrifice. Men marry to have their wives bless their corpses before they are buried. We all need eternal happiness, Drissa. Now I will not get your blessings and neither will you receive mine. When our children die young, they become God's angels, and they are the ones who are sent by God to pour icy water on their parents' heads when we melt under the eternal burning sun.
Drissa screams.

It will take a man's whole life, Drissa. We will stand there awaiting trial before God. When that day comes, the sun will melt defiant souls. There will be no water, no rain, no food and the grass will be as sharp as blades. Men will groan and cry for mercy. Who will plead for you? Tell me, who will ask God to forgive you? Now that I have lost that husband, my children will pour cold water from heaven on my head. They will comfort me and wipe my tears and sing songs of happiness. You wanted the whole world and now you've lost everything.

DRISSA
Will you not save me? Will you not pity your husband?

GHOST
Angrily.
Husband? You a husband? No, not for what you did. The angels will pull you down to where the live fire will roast you like dust in a sand storm. Do you remember what happened under the kola nut tree?

DRISSA
Claps his hands.
The kola nut tree?

GHOST
Now you can't remember.

DRISSA
I was crowned chief, you see. Besides, I prayed for your salvation.

GHOST
> *Bitterly.*

Salvation! God have mercy. Salvation? My daughter slaughtered like a goat on banana leaves. To fulfill the empty prophecies of those marabout[21] men that until you raped your own daughter, you would never be chief of Kissy. First you raped Fatimah, she was not your real daughter. And in fear of not winning the election, you took my own daughter Abbi; your own blood raped her and tortured her to death. In fear of my suspicions, you ordered your slaves to kill me. What benefit did you get by killing me and my daughter? Again you stand on the edge of misery.

> *The lights go out and the ghost leaves the stage. The stage lights brighten. Drissa rises in senseless fury.*

DRISSA

Come back here! I paid the bride price. Now out! Huh? So... there, under the kola nut tree.

> *Drissa runs offstage and returns with a collection of road signs.*
>
> *Much confused and frightened.*

Where is she? I am chief of this place! I Drissa! I Drissa! I Drissa Bangura!

> *He begins to put the road signs on the stage so that the audience may see them.*

What is written on this? "No Exit." Good, there will be no way out now. She is trapped.

> *Picks up another.*

What is on this?

---

[21] **Marabout men.** Professional students of the Koran, who give prophecies. (pronounces maraboo`)

Reads it aloud.

"Dynamite, keep away." Do you hear? Keep away!

Picks up another.

What's on this? "Ghosts and spirits not allowed." Ha! What's on this "Walk away!" Walk away?

After a short pause, he returns to his corner, muttering. "The end. The everlasting. The dreadful end." The stage lights are now steady and bright. After an awkward silence, Pabuya and a POLICEMAN, dressed in a jumped suit and carrying a heavy stick and handcuffs, are seen standing stage right. They whisper to one another.

PABUYA

On his toes, a finger on his lips, whispering to the policeman.

Na woman. She always cam' here to disturb people na market.

POLICEMAN

He must be a man. All the mad women dey na Mental Hospital.

PABUYA

Man go wear red frock? Na woman! Na for tie am hand en foot. You nor know say one mad woman kill one nurse one time? Mad woman nar danger.

Pulls his mouth scornfully and with hands behind his back.

Na true, Sir: Dis worl' do for fraid.[22]

POLICEMAN

There is no other way we can get him. You tiptoe quietly and

---

[22] **dis worl' do for fraid.** "This world's enough to frighten you."

collect those signs; if he falls on you, I will help you strike upon him like thunder and lightning!

Voices are heard offstage.

PABUYA
Trying to place the voices.
Na people dem dey cam so. You hear? Dis na wahala!

POLICEMAN
It won't be safe for them. Quietly go across there and stop them. Tell them to wait for a while because there is a dangerous mad woman around.

Pabuya tiptoes across the stage, covering his mouth. Appearing are ABASS, carrying his briefcase, Baimbadi carrying Abass' suitcase, and Pastor Brown following behind.

ABASS
So this is the way things stand—in Freetown. I tell you, Freetown is not yet Free!! What has this damned country become? A hell on earth?

PABUYA
Springing to his feet and silencing Abass.
Shh-shh-shh! Danger!

PASTOR BROWN
Ignoring him.
Danger! Don't mind him, he is a market beggar. Do you think you can fool us?

They all start off again, but Pabuya bars their way.

38

PABUYA
In a tearful and pleading voice.
Believe me, sir. E nor safe for wun'am na dis market.

ABASS
Surprised.
Why not? Is this not a public place?

PABUYA
Danger dey wait for wuna-e dey under dat table. Crazy people nor ba done na Salone!

BAIMBADI
Advancing forward.
A woman? Nonsense!

PABUYA
See am! Na'imdey whistle so, danger woman.

BAIMBADI
A woman whistles? A woman!
Seeing the policeman.
There is the police.
Shouting.
Police!

PABUYA
Jumps furiously.
No. No, please. Na danger woman!
Drissa begins to sing aloud.

DRISSA

Fire, fire, fire mama,
Fire dey cam.
I want to see my loving wife,
Loving wife I love so well.
Fire, fire, fire baby-yoh!
Fire dey cam.
Pompodi! Kiddi pompom!

> As he finishes singing, Drissa begins to dance medita-
> tively. Pabuya signals the police. The policeman beckons
> him to collect the sign posts. Pabuya starts off and then
> stops, scrutinizing the road signs.

ABASS

Perplexed.

What type of a mad woman does such crazy things?

> *Pabuya begins to pick up the road signs. Drissa, seeing
> Pabuya screams and rises furiously form his corner.*

DRISSA

Stay! Set it down! I say set it down!

PASTOR BROWN

Almost screaming.

Baimbadi. He is your brother!

ABASS

Softly to Baimbadi and with teeth firmly clenched.

Uncle Drissa.

DRISSA

After a long pause. Rises from the corner behind the table, carefully examines the men around him, advances towards Abass and embraces him in a tearful voice, almost on the verge of tears.

Abass! Abass! Abass, my son!

ABASS

Drissa! Uncle Drissa!

Abass and Drissa embrace warmly; Abass in tears.

Oh, uncle. Uncle, what has happened to you?

DRISSA

Now releasing Abass.

You are such a fine boy. I am cold, my son. I have no one to take care of me. no one.

To Baimbadi, who is lost in thought.

Why? Why did we do it?

ABASS

Sharply to Baimbadi.

What did you do?

BAIMABADI

Shrugging off the thought.

Me? I don't know.

ABASS

Do you expect me to know or answer his question? Your brother is having a nervous breakdown; he is exhausted and losing his senses. Do you expect him to know himself? Why didn't you take him to Kissy Mental Hospital? Why?

> *Baimbadi is dripping wet with sweat and keeps wiping his face with a red cloth.*

Is that all you do when asked? Wiping your face with a red velvet cloth! You are really a wonderful brother.

PASTOR BROWN

Now, now, Abass, you must not talk to your father like this.

ABASS

Nonsense, Pastor. His brother is having a nervous breakdown—

POLICEMAN

Then we must take him to the Kissy Mental Hospital.

BAIMBADI

The Kissy Mental Hospital? No, the man is seriously ill. He's bewitched!

ABASS

Drissa will be taken to the mental hospital. There is nothing the hospital will not cure. There's nothing white people cannot do! Bewitched? We will know who's the devil when we get him there!

BAIMBADI

> *Taking off his shoes and carrying them in his hands, in a tearful voice...*

Abass, my son, can't you understand? Drissa does not need the help of those doctors at the Kissy Mental Hospital. The man is bewitched because of his wealth and power. Evil spells have been cast upon him—this is witchcraft!

ABASS
Still holding Drissa in his arms.
Witchcraft? Nonsense! What do you know about witchcraft?

BAIMBADI
Taking off his white gown.
You must understand, my child. We must not allow the whole town to know about this—

ABASS
Dragging Drissa offstage, stops, and sharply to Baimbadi.
To hell with the town! Drissa does not need the town. He needs some rest. He is only having a nervous breakdown. The hospital is the best place for him.

BAIMBADI
Beating his shoe on the floor and beckoning to the sky.
Oh, you up there! Hear him? You spite me, child? You disrespect me?

PASTOR BROWN
Abass, you must listen to your father.
Drissa begins to dance quietly and sings "Fire, fire mama."

PABUYA
Bursting into laughter.
E dey sing "fire, fire." E go burn the whole market with his "fire, fire:" Take him now, take him away—Kissy Mental next stop!

Drissa is dragged offstage. Before they leave stage, the policeman attempts handcuffing Drissa, but Abass disapproves of it.

ABASS
Almost in tears.
No, you need not do that. He will be all right in my hands.
To Pastor and Pabuya.
Pastor, please bring the briefcase along. Give the suitcase to Pabuya.

Abass and the policeman begin to drag Drissa offstage. Drissa begins to feel his way like a chameleon.

DRISSA
Quietly.
What place is this, children? Are we lost?

ABASS
After a long pause.
No, uncle, everything will be all right.

DRISSA
To Abass.
Hold my right hand.
To the policeman.
And you, hold my left hand.

They slowly drag Drissa offstage, while Pastor Brown and Pabuya follow behind. Baimbadi is rooted to his feet, lost in thought. Then a continuous, threatening knocking is heard off-stage.

DRISSA
Frightened.
What noise is that?

PASTOR BROWN
The noise of women.

DRISSA
Trembling.
No, they are coming for me.

ABASS
No one is coming.

DRISSA
Screams as he is dragged offstage.
Scorpions! Snakes! Crabs! I paid the bride price!
> *All leave, except Baimbadi. The lights now begin to shower on Baimbadi. Still holding his shoes in his left hand and gown in his right hand.*

BAIMBADI
Kneeling helplessly at front of stage.
Drissa, is this the end?
> *Facing the audience. An awkward silence.*

Is this the end, Drissa? When you came home that night and said to me: "Brother Baimbadi, the chieftaincy will be ours." And all the blood spilled on the ground.
> *Pause.*

Is this where it led to? And when I revealed my dream that I saw you carried in a hammock with a shaved head... and in the sacred bush, didn't you overpower all the other contestants in that dream? Where was I wrong?

> *Still kneeling down, assumes a position as if he is ready to pray. Then enter Nene and Fatimah, stage left. Nene in a thin white velvet gown, and Fatimah in her sacrificial gown.*

FATIMAH
Whispering.
Auntie, your husband is praying.
> *They stand still and listen.*

NENE
Shocked.
Shh! Oh, Baimbadi, you have it all wrong. That is not the right way to pray. The sun does not rise in the north, it rises in the east, and when men pray they face the east.

BAIMBADI
Slowly rising and walking away toward stage right.
Where? We killed Makalay and her daughter Abbi as sacrifice for the chieftaincy. Were you not crowned chief? Where was I wrong? Now you deny my help. Was I wrong then?
> *Leaving stage. Nene, in an uncontrollable fury, pulls Fatimah towards her.*

NENE
It is all out, now!

FATIMAH
What's out, Auntie?

NENE
Pulling her by the left ear. Fatimah screams.
What? Witch! Have you forgotten how my sister took you away from that village of witches?
Breathless.
And... saved your life? Didn't you hear this poor man confessing?

FATIMAH
Softly.
I...only...
Mumbles.

NENE
Releases her, angrily.
I cannot hear you. You! You!
Pinching her cheek.
You will die. You will die, and you will drag our family to the grave. But I tell you now—it will be out. It will be out. Listen to me.

FATIMAH
Now very frightened.
Yes, Auntie.

NENE
In a pathetic tone of voice.
You! Look me in the face. It is you that will make this hidden thing come to light.
Fatimah with mouth wide open.
Yes, look at me!

Fatimah trembles.

You stand there with your mouth wide open... Didn't you hear Baimbadi confessing that he and Drissa killed my sister, Makalay, and her daughter, Abbi, in order to win the chieftaincy? The death of Makalay remains a mystery to us. Abbi's dead body was never brought home for burial. And When Baimbadi and Drissa took you away to Kamasondo, didn't they keep you away for three days?

FATIMAH
Trembling, with her mouth wide open.
But, Auntie, I came home the fourth day.

NENE
Yes. Yes. You came back the fourth day. You came home and fell ill. Have you forgotten how you nearly died?
Fatimah does not answer.
Answer me!
Fatimah only nods in affirmation.
Now look me right in the face. Baimbadi has planned your wedding to take Place next week. See, see; now you tremble. I say, either you tell it all or you will die. My son Saidu will not marry you. Will not marry a chicken slaughtered because it was deathly sick. That chicken will not enter the guts of my own son to poison and kill him.

FATIMAH
Almost in tears.
Nothing, nothing happened to me.

NENE
Angrily.
What! Nothing? Didn't I see you bleeding between your legs,
and—sitting in the sun searching for warmth like a bewitched
child?

FATIMAH
It was the journey, Auntie.

NENE
Viciously, threatening her.
The journey? Liar! Fatimah, we all depend on you to speak.
You must tell the truth. You see, if you can only speak out,
the whole crime will be out.

FATIMAH
Now weeping.
Auntie. They will kill me.

NENE
In confusion.
Who will? Look, we will protect you, nothing will happen to
you, my child. Do you want to die?

FATIMAH
Still weeping.
No, Auntie. I want my life. I want to live. I want to live...

NENE
Relaxed.
Then you must tell it—tell everything. My sister Makalay,

had appeared to me in my sleep. I have it here...in my palm.
You know it.

> FATIMAH
> *Trembling.*

They...they...made me drink...
> *Pause.*

blood!

> NENE
> *Dancing with rage.*

Blood! Who did? What blood?

> FATIMAH
> *Silent, not wanting to speak; then says,*

Blood—they gave me some fresh water drawn from a sacred
well and Kola nuts mixed with Abbi's blood.
> *Trembling.*

They said to me, "if you tell what you saw to anyone, you will
die with a swollen stomach!"

> NENE

They did that to you?

> FATIMAH

Please, Auntie, pray for me now.
> *Trembling with the chicken in her hands.*

Pray for me—the needles are piercing my body. My guts are
all shattered!!
> *Wanting to faint. Nene grabs her and presses her against
> her bosom.*

NENE
Shocked.
What! The child is murdered!

BLACK OUT

Act Two

Why on the very threshold of life do we become dull, grey, uninteresting, lazy, indifferent, useless, unhappy? Our town has been going on for two hundred years—there are a hundred thousand people living in it; and there is not one saint in the past, or the present, not one man of learning, not one artist, not one man in the least remarkable who could inspire envy or a passionate desire to imitate him...They only eat, drink, sleep, and then die... Others are born, and they also eat, drink, and sleep, and not to be bored to stupefaction they vary their lives by nasty gossip, vodka, cards, litigation; and the wives deceive their husbands, and the husbands tell lies and pretend that they see and hear nothing, and an overwhelming vulgar influence weighs upon the children, and the divine spark is quenched in them and they become the same sort of pitiful, dead creatures, all exactly alike, as their fathers and mothers...

— Anton Chekhov, *Three Sisters*

Scene One

A few hours later. On the same day. Saturday. Nene's room. There is a movable back wall. Hanging on this wall are framed pictures of Nene's twin sister, Makalay. The pictures are turned against the wall. In one of the framed pictures are Makalay, her daughter Abbi, and Fatimah. The framed pictures are covered over with white satin. Nene is mourning the loss of her sister, although she is also expecting her educated son, Abass. She is seen sitting quietly and in her native white gown. Fatimah sits beside her, also in her sacrificial gown of white, red, and black. Before the scene opens, a swift and furious roll of drums, in a rising and falling wave. Then, as the drums die away, the light begins to glow, clear and bright. Nene rises quietly and begins to hum a dirge in Arabic: "La-ela ela-la," as she fingers her prayer beads. Then footsteps are heard. Nene quietly advances backstage as Saidu enters center stage, dressed in khaki shirt and shorts, his head shaved, and carrying a sparrow in a cage. He is very jubilant and energetic. Sets the cage down at center stage and begins to address it.

SAIDU
Excitedly clapping and addressing the sparrow.
Ah! Look! Look at me! Hey! Whistle! Whistle, now, now!
Cheerfully.
I say whistle, sparrow! Whistle for your master.
Laughs rudely.
Aye! I'll soon give you up. You know that. Fatimah will soon take your place. I'll no longer sing for you and play with you...

As he turns toward the house, Nene quickly withdraws, bewildered and shocked at her son's behavior. Voices are heard offstage. Nene rises, listening. Saidu is fixed to the spot. As he turns, he sees Pastor Brown, Abass and Pabuya. Abass is still dressed in his black suit. Pabuya is carrying Abass' suitcase, and the Pastor is carrying the briefcase. Saidu runs to meet them, grabs Abass' right hand, and the two exchange profuse greetings, while the Pastor and Pabuya watch with excitement; still shaking Abass' hand.

Abass! Abass! Abass—little one. Hey! Huh? You've grown into a man. See your beard. What! Did Father see you with that bearded face? You must shave that beard. Children must not grow beard when the old ones are baldheaded.

ABASS
I will shave it. I will shave it.

SAIDU
You must. See?
Takes off his cap.

PASTOR BROWN
Pleased with Saidu's attitude.
See what I was telling you, Abass!

SAIDU
Releases Abass' hand and quickly takes Pastor Brown's hand.
Oh, Pastor, I didn't see you. Pastor, do you think Abass is still a good Muslim?
Sharply to Abass.
No pork meat has touched your lips?

> *Turning again to Pastor Brown.*

We need to take him to the sacred river and wash him clean, so that he'll be like us again. You look so different.

> *Abass is laughing throughout.*

Oh. I see you're laughing. I'm really serious.

ABASS
> *Changing the topic.*

Where is Mother?

SAIDU
> *Not listening.*

Where is Father?

ABASS
> *Now scrutinizing the compound.*

Is this the new compound?

SAIDU
> *Energetically. Pastor Brown is amused; Pabuya is also observing and laughs from time to time.*

Yes! This is the new compound. Remember the old one—thick bushes, coconut trees here and there. Mango trees, orange trees—it used to be full of children. Visitors are always knocking on the door or sending greetings. It was full of life, and noisy

> *Pause. With arms wide open.*

But this is different. Uncle Drissa, Father and I cut down all the trees. No more snakes, rabbits, monkeys. Just us. The family and visitors who come to see father and mother.

PASTOR BROWN

This must be a good place to be. You can study here without anyone bothering you.

SAIDU

In a state of bravado and jubilation, takes his brother's hands and both embrace warmly. Pabuya and Pastor Brown shake hands as well.

Pastor! Allah is wonderful! Huh? Ah! Ah-ah-ah-ah-ah-Allah is great.

Turns to Pastor Brown.

What do you think of him, Pastor? With such a big stomach like a pregnant woman?

PASTOR BROWN

Quickly.

That's African dignity! A big stomach shows you're healthy and prosperous! That's African dignity.

They all laugh.

PABUYA

Na fine man. Fine, fine man.

PASTOR BROWN

We must go in and greet Nene. She must be in her room.

As they move towards Nene's room.

Everyone is waiting to see you! The whole town is waiting to receive you! Allah!

Nene comes out and stands in the doorway.

SAIDU
Shouting.
Nene! Nene! A big stranger. Abass is here!
> *Nene takes off her shoes in jubilation and runs to meet Abass. Embraces her son and begins to dance, fanning him with her head tie. Fatimah stands in the doorway, watching in amusement.*

NENE
> *She bows before her son and sings "The Song of the Doe Rescued by the Women."*

Uhngpa wawr uh buhkee su!
Uh-wonee me kanay mu.
Uhng pa wawr uh buhkee su.
Uhng pa wawr men wong de Deebeeyah,
Ta sawmra angbai a-kande.
A day pa su t' t' kaw.
Oh, yayow, Almami Sorie.
Ta Kanay anglan-gbah
Tung tayow! Oh, tan-taye eppahye!
S'bow rah k-nambuhrah.
Aw-war maw woor ro ruhrayn gay,
Ruh bomnga ang tang kahkaw.
Uhngt'n ka kanday dayray,
Taw pa, "Gbuhpe! Moontha ba kaw,
Ng t'kuhrh eppah."
Uhngpa wawr uh buhkee su!
Uhwoneee me kanay mu,
Uhngpa wawr uh buhkee su!
Oh! I'm so happy. I'm so happy.
> *Turns to Pastor Brown.*

When he was young, he never wanted to sleep in my room. He was always complaining about kriffis, genii: "I see a devil in your room, Nene." Always dreaming about strange things. Do you believe in dreams now that you are full grown? Or don't the white people believe in anything?

ABASS

They do. Some do believe in dreams. Maybe I do. Dreams? Oh, Mother. You always see me as the frightened little baby—now I don't accept just anything as true. My education has taught me to always question things, even the existence of God.

SAIDU
Sharply to Abass.
You! You, Abass!

NENE

What country is it again—Ka-England?

SAIDU

Ka-Englen. Mother.
Pastor Brown and Pabuya laugh.

NENE

Sometimes I used to think I would never see you again.

PASTOR BROWN

That's the wonder of God.

NENE
Takes off her head tie.
I have grown old.

ABASS

No, Mother; you are still young.

NENE

I just want to show you my grey hair, though not as old as
the Pastor.

PASTOR BROWN

No, Nene. A man of God is never old. My hair is grey, but
my spirit is with the Lord. A religious man, like me, is not
afraid of death...

NENE

*An awkward silence. Then, remembering the death of
her sister and niece, on the verge of tears.*

Oh, my son. I wish...if only...

ABASS

Comforting her.

Now, Nene. Don't cry. I am here to stay.

PASTOR BROWN

Abass, take her in. Go in with her. I will wait outside for
Baimbadi.

FATIMAH

Welcome, brother Abass.

ABASS

Surprised at recognizing Fatimah.

Fatimah! Fatimah! What a surprise, huh? Everyone has grown

up. Except Saidu—

SAIDU
Protesting as they all laugh.
Oh, never mind my height.

ABASS
To Nene.
Now sit quietly, mother. I swear I will stay now. Let me give some money to the old man.
Calling from within.
Old Pa!

SAIDU
Calling.
Pabuya!
Pabuya comes in.

ABASS
Here, take this.
Gives Pabuya some money.

PABUYA
Kisses the money and bites each coin as he gently puts it in his pocket.
Thank you! Thank you! Thank you berri much.
Pabuya holds Abass' hands, leading him to stage front; puts the money in his pocket.
Pastor, close you eye. Devil pikin.[1] See son. Them neighbor

---

[1] **Pikin.** Child.

61

them jealous an' Kongosha.[2] Be careful. You do good, 'cause the hospital, na the best place for Drissa.

Shakes his head violently and holds up his finger.

Neighbor nor good—oh! Them take this, en'take that; cut ya, en' put ya. If you shit you pants, don't make them see you. If you wet you pants, don't let them see ya. All na the same—three en-ten-pence. Me like you, that's why me warn you. You hear? Be careful.

SAIDU

Abass! Mother wants you here!

ABASS

Yes! I'm coming.

Pabuya tiptoes across stage left, holding his right pocket with both hands.

PASTOR BROWN

To Abass.

Tell your mother that I have gone to meet her husband.

Pastor leaves stage right.

SAIDU

I must go too. I must go and prepare the room. From today my brother will share the room with me.

Saidu leaves.

NENE

Controlling her feelings.

Sit here, Abass. Sit! Sit, my child. I want you to tell me about

---

[2] **Kongosahg.** Gossip.

those wonderful white people. Tell me, Abass, is it too difficult to live there? You without a mother to take care of you.

ABASS

It's a rough world, Mother. You take a real beating, living in those countries. To be there one must decide to live first. In England, I lived in London. That's the capital of their country, like Freetown. City life is rough, Mother. I was broke. I had to take different jobs. I washed dishes; I cooked; I drove trucks—any job that was handy. But I was lucky to have a scholarship. I believe in hard work, Mother. Remember what you used to tell me: "Be nice to people and they will be nice to you too." That was my precept!

NENE

Who prepared your meals? White people are wonderful! They do impossible things—they are devils.

Long pause.

ABASS

No, Mother; the white people believe in hard work. They believe in themselves—we black people don't.

Pause.

White people worship work! But we are taught to hate work; to fear life and love death. That's why we pray all the time. See what's becoming of Saidu. He is not even forty and he looks like sixty. He prays all the time. Can a man who prays all the time know the pain of life?

NENE

You will help him to change his ways.

ABASS

Saidu? If only he could stop and think about life. But he goes about praying; telling old tales to women and dreaming about the Messiah. Mother, we are not pictures on walls. We have lives and we must make the best of them. Sometimes, I think our minds have ceased to exist. I'll find him a job when I have settled down.

NENE

What did you study? They told me you are now a doctor. Do you operate upon dead people?

ABASS
Smiles.

Not that type of doctor. I treat people who are mentally disturbed. Those who are sick in the mind.

NENE
After a long pause.

How about those who are sick in the body? Do you treat them too?

ABASS

Sometimes.
To Fatimah.

Please, Fatimah, give me some water.
Fatimah leaves.

Nene, what is happening to Uncle Drissa? Why didn't you write about it? I look like a stranger in my own home. I have the feeling that something is knocking my heart almost to pieces.
Softly, almost whispering.

What has happened to Fatimah? Why does she drag her feet as she walks? She is not sick, is she?

NENE

My son, we are all sick.
Long pause.
The burdens of the past were too heavy; but the ones of the present are over-crushing. We may have to bear these burdens until the day we are buried.

ABASS

But life has to change. We can't go on this way. You are not as young as you used to be, and I am not either. We have to grow from the past.

NENE

Where will the change come from? We change our clothes every day. We want beautiful clothes—we wear caftans, we wear boubous,[3] and big gowns, and we look different every minute. But do our minds match that beauty to which we pretend? That's the frightening thing, my son. Many things have changed but not for the better.

ABASS

After a long pause.
But things must not go on like this. See what has become of your son, Saidu, and Uncle Drissa. And see what is happening to your foster daughter, Fatimah. Where is your sister Makalay, and Abbi?

---

3 **Boubou.** A flowing gown. (Pronounced boobah).

NENE

That, also, I will talk to you about. We live in a world that ter-
rifies all of us. I fear for you and the unborn child. I am now
nearly seventy. I know where I have come from...

Pauses.

But do we know where we are going? Do we?

*Long pause. Then Fatimah reenters with a cup of water
and bows courteously to Abass.*

ABASS

Thanks, my dear child.

*Abass drinks, hands her the empty cup, and watches her
fixedly as she takes it, ready to leave.*

NENE

Calling to Fatimah.

Fatimah, go get the kitchen ready for cooking. I know the
stranger is hungry.

Clapping her hands.

From today, I'll prepare your meals and wash your clothes, hm?

ABASS

Staring fixedly at Fatimah as she leaves.

Maybe she is sick.

NENE

No, sit. There is one thing I want to tell you. You are my son,
and I must not hide anything from you. There are deep holes
covered with dry banana leaves in this compound.

ABASS

At a loss.

What are you talking about?

NENE

You see that picture covered with white satin? Go and un-cover it.

Abass does so.

ABASS

Oh, Nene, this must be Auntie Makalay and Abbi?

Still holding the picture.

Where are they, Nene? Why didn't they come to meet me?

NENE

Still controlled; long pause.

She would if she were here. Both are dead.

ABASS

Springs to his feet.

Dead! Dead! Dead! Oh, Nene. Impossible!

NENE

That's why I said there are deep holes around here. I see you want to jump when you are to crawl. A child that crawls lives longer.

Abass falls on the bed weeping.

Now listen to me. Abass, do you hear? Now sit and listen to me. There was a hunter whose brilliance and skills surpassed the gods'. One day, this man decided to hunt elephants in-stead of deer. His fame for killing elephants spread far and wide. He killed elephants every day. One day, the elephants held a meeting to discuss how to trap him. One of the elephants turned into a beautiful woman, and this woman went to visit the hunter. She stayed with him for some days and then asked him to marry her. The hunter agreed. During her visit, she learned a lot about shooting elephants. Before she left, the woman in turn invited the hunter to visit her parents, as is the custom. The following day, the hunter packed all his belongings. But before they left, the hunter's mother sent her voice across the room: "Look closely under her ankles," she said, "Do her feet resemble those of a human being? Burn the gun powder, and you'll find out." The hunter did so. Elephants hate the smell of gunpowder. The woman ran into the bush and never returned.

    Pause.

ABASS

What does this mean, Mother?

NENE
Severely to Abass.
Trust no one. No one! Talk a little and keep the rest to yourself. Do you hear?

ABASS
Perplexed.
Even you? But—

NENE
Listen, my child... My sister was warned but didn't listen to me. Two months ago... before she died... we went to the funeral of Pamamudu, and there a crab slowly crept in and bit Makalay; no one saw it.

ABASS

Ready to collapse in disbelief.

A crab! A crab! A crab in a house? A crab bit her? — But Nene—what has a crab got to do with Auntie Makalay's death?

NENE

Bursts into tears; then enter Baimbadi and Pastor Brown.

The crab came to warn her, but...

PASTOR BROWN

What is the matter with her? Why is she crying? Abass, your friends are coming to visit you... Why is she crying?

Then Saidu is heard praying outside.

SAIDU

Ala-hu Akbar

Ala-hu Akbar

Ala-hu Akbar.

The lights fade out.

Scene Two

The family compound. As the light comes up, the family has just had dinner. It is now six in the evening. Abass, Pastor Brown, Baimbadi and Saidu are sitting on a mat; a big bowl is in the center. Stage right are a couple of chairs and a table. Baimbadi belches heavily and rises.

BAIMBADI
A little at ease with his son, though not with Nene. Speaks authoritatively.

Now, Abass. This is the compound we have built for you. What have you brought us?

ABASS
Without interest. He has perceived something ominous, but is very confused and bewildered.

Father, you know I could have stayed overseas if I'd wanted to. But it wouldn't be wise to do so. The family needs me. My country needs me. I am more vital and useful here. There is a lot we need to do here, Father. There is a lot, I tell you...

Long pause. Baimbadi is walking up and down, proud of his son, but deeply worried within.

If all should stay abroad, who will say: "This is my native land?" And who will dare to say, on his death bed, "I gave my whole life to my country. I was loyal, faithful. I never took a penny from the poor. Now my dust will be honored as I die in my native land."

To his father.

I tell you, Father, not many of us will dare utter those words. There are many of my type—educated, young, ready to help.

But where are they? They are afraid to come. You know why? Everybody in this country is a crook, a murderer, or a thief. I am here because I've often asked myself: "if we all stay overseas, whose continent is it? Whose country is it?" That's why I came running home. My country, my family, and my duty to my countrymen. But the help starts with you yourself. They all talk of changing this—

BAIMBADI
Interrupting, emphatically.
Son, the mark of a young man must be deeds, not only words. You've shown us how we ought to behave. Some talk like parrots—wawa,wawa, waa. The change starts with you. You cannot make better human beings of others if you have not become better yourself.
Laughs and shakes his head.
You see, tortoise and elephant once sought to improve their speed. The tortoise said, "I'll cure you of this sickness."
Holding his stick in the air.
You know what the elephant said? "First, apply the medicine to yourself," he said. "When I see with my own eyes, then I will be your patient." How can you help others if you are helpless?
Long pause.
Pastor, what do you think?

PASTOR BROWN
Pleased with father-son relationship.
I'm happy to see both of you talk like that. I'm really happy. Father and son are one flesh and blood. I'm deeply touched.
To Abass.

I'm proud of you, Abass. I am very proud of you.

ABASS
With some curiosity.
Father, why didn't you write about Uncle Drissa, Auntie Makalay, and her daughter? It is your duty, Father. Why didn't you warn me about all these things?

BAIMBADI
Becoming angry
What are you talking about? What do you mean? To be writing letters about death in the family—

ABASS
Mother—

BAIMBADI
Oh, is that it? Nene is telling you—
Abass and Baimbadi face each other. Saidu, perplexed, comes between them. Pastor Brown tries to stop them.
You want to slap your father? Is this your gift that you've brought us?

PASTOR BROWN
Pleading, and pressing Abass' hands warmly.
Abass, son; you need a little rest, hm? Don't believe whatever your mother tells you. We all will die some day; the Bible tells us so. Your friends are coming to greet you. You must be cheerful. Don't allow them to know what's in your heart. Your father is your father. Why are you fighting? It was beginning to feel like the good old days again. Why must you fight?

ABASS

Why didn't you warn me about all these things? Why?

PASTOR BROWN

Listen, all roads have curves. Things have to happen: if God's only son should suffer death, who will not! My son, when the tallest tree in the bush falls, all the little ones will wither away.

Footsteps are heard offstage.

That must be one of your friends. We will talk about these things later—

JOSHUA enters. A tall, lanky man in his thirties. He is dressed in a dark suit, rumpled but well kept. He keeps several pens in his front pocket. He moves with grace and buoyancy—a sign of confidence. Abass rises and both men shake hands.

ABASS

My oh my! Joshua! When was the last time we met in London? Now it's in Sierra Leone. How are you, Papa-Boy?

JOSHUA

Oh, quite well...Almamy Brukus told me you have come—

ABASS

Almamy Brukus? He is in town?

JOSHUA

As a matter of fact, we were to come together, but he decided to buy a chicken for you, to greet the stranger.

73

ABASS
Laughs.
A chicken! Not even a goat? Come and meet my father.
To Joshua, with difficulty.
This is my father. And this is your old teacher, Pastor
Brown.

JOSHUA
Hides a smile.
Oh yes, I know Pastor. I'll never forget him.

PASTOR BROWN
To Joshua
Sit down, Mister Pens...
To Abass.
Joshua is very punctual. He comes to church every Sunday—

JOSHUA
No, Pastor. Not every Sunday. I have been ill for a while.

PASTOR BROWN
That's a bad sign, to be sick. Are you aware of any sin you've
committed since then?

JOSHUA
I am not a sinner, Pastor. No one here has the face of a murderer, or a rapist or a thief. I'm a proper Christian.

PASTOR BROWN
I see. I see. But don't forget your church dues.

BAIMBADI
In a fatherly tone.
How about you, Abass? Did you pray five times every day while you were in England?

ABASS
I didn't need to. Besides, I never had the time.

BAIMBADI
Never had the time?

PASTOR BROWN
Rising.
What is this world coming to? You two are sinners.

SAIDU
Turns to Baimbadi.
You must do something to bring them to the house of God. They must be whipped.

ABASS
I thanked God in my heart; I don't have to pray five times a day.

BAIMBADI
Angrily.
Abass! We must go to the mosque next Friday and ask the old Muslims to pray for you. To ask Allah to forgive you and all your sins. Don't you see my forehead? There's a black spot on my forehead because I pray every hour. We must not forget Allah.

PASTOR BROWN
Almost speechless.
This is inconceivable—inconceivable—

JOSHUA
Pastor, the world we used to know while we were overseas is different from this. Here, people sleep till sunrise. They go to bed when they like. In England, a man has to fight for his existence. There is too severe a struggle for existence. God will understand if a man failed to go to church... England is a different world; entirely different.

BAIMBADI
Angrily.
Foolish thoughts. So no one prays there. They don't know anything about God? Allah sees everything, knows everything, and hears everything. He will come down upon you like lightning in a thunder storm. No more of these foolish thoughts! You and the White man are sinners.

ABASS
Joshua didn't say that. God is everywhere. Even Moses found out from God that all ground is holy. There are people who have time to pray, I never said I never prayed, only that I never had the time to pray five times every day. I had to live and survive. Maybe I'll find time here where people pray fifty times an hour and yet have barely to eat.

ALMAMY BRUKKUS is seen entering stage left. He is short but dignified, broad chested, and has a deep and melodious voice, almost that of a praise singer. He is a

health inspector. He wears white hose up to the knees,
stuffed with all kinds of pens, a pair of white drill shorts,
and a short-sleeved white shirt with pens in the front
pocket. He wears a khaki helmet. His speech is quick,
and he perspires a lot, wiping his face frequently with a
handkerchief. In his right hand is a portfolio. He walks
briskly to meet Abass, followed by Pabuya, who carries a
white cockerel and is raggedly dressed.

ABASS
Man Brukus!

BRUKUS
That's me, boy. What a world! If only it's like this in that
place...
    Joshua looks at Pastor Brown.
God's kingdom. Where old friends will meet and be happy.
Boy! You've grown taller.

ABASS
So have you. It's one of God's wonders.

PASTOR BROWN
    A finger on his lips; with disbelief.
God be praised! For once, I have heard him thank God.

BRUKUS
    Shaking hands with everyone.
Oh, Pastor Brown. When did I last see you? At the funeral of
Pamamudu, hm?
    Slight pause; to Abass.

I brought you the chicken. Pabuya, take the chicken to Nene.

PABUYA
Comes forward and salutes everyone; bows courteously before Pastor Brown.
I nor go forget this man. Na'im get for pray pa me dead body.
Leaves.

PASTOR BROWN
Delighted.
He's a man of God, that one.

BAIMBADI
Rises.
Pastor, let's give the young men a chance to talk, hm? Let's go and keep Nene's company.
Pastor Brown, Baimbadi and Saidu all leave. As they leave, Brukus laughs rudely.

JOSHUA
What's funny?

BRUKUS
The Pastor. Don't you see the way he walks, like a saint. Proudly bearing the burden of the cross. What a man!

JOSHUA
I will never understand Pastor Brown.

BRUKUS
He's a wily one that Pastor. Ten years ago, he was a Catholic;

then a Protestant, then a Baptist, then a Jehovah's Witness.

JOSHUA
Interrupting.
A Protestant-Catholic-Baptist-Evangelical United Brethren-Son of Jehovah and what is he now?

ABASS
Laughs.
And what is he now?

BRUKUS
Just a preacher. The Bible is his passport. Two years ago, he was almost converted to the Islamic faith. He wanted to marry a second wife, and the Catholic Church said no. He didn't find salvation with Jehovah's Witnesses either. So his first wife left him.
Whispering.
I heard that he's dead here...
Pointing.
Here.

JOSHUA
You mean he's impotent?

BRUKUS
Exactly. He cannot do anything with a woman. You know how he used to beat us—"Obey your teacher!" Remember his history lessons? Early man and that stuff.
All laugh.

ABASS

Early man teaching about early man.

BRUKUS

Spelling and then pronouncing the words. ABASS and JOSHUA join him.

A-T, at; T-O, to; G-O, go; C-A-T, cat; P-A-N, pan. All that rubbish. I didn't understand a thing.

Pause.

So, you've now returned home, finally?

ABASS

Oh, yes. I've come to join you. Thanks again for the chicken.

BRUKUS

Oh, don't mention it.

JOSHUA

Did they kill today?—I mean the butchers...

BRUKUS

After a long pause.

Yes, they have good meat today. Of course, I don't have to buy any meat. That's the damn good thing about being a health inspector. As soon as I appear with my white uniform—all hands on deck! "The health inspector is here! Give way to the health inspector." They'll part like waves in stormy Weather. I'll take off my khaki helmet and you known what? I don't have to say a word. The helmet speaks for me! "Meat! More meat for the inspector." What a job!

JOSHUA

Your mere presence is a threat to them.

BRUKUS

No! It isn't. They need me, and I need them: "you chop, me chop; palaver finish."[4]

ABASS

That's bribery.

BRUKUS

Damn me, if I deny their offer. Do you know how I got this job, Abass? It's not just papers, education or credentials—put for them.[5] you know the phrase here—"put for me" or "see to see." When you walk into that damn employment office, you'll hear strange ways of speaking. People there speak a language that you'll never understand. Not complete sentences but queer phrases: "Put for me." "See to see." "Can dey nor." "Rob-hand." All queer things. What do you expect of me, a little man? Hey, boss; I'll take everything.

JOSHUA

He's right. If those at the top ask for "see to see," as the phrase implies, why not Brukus? A tied goat that doesn't eat the grass around it is one dead goat.

BRUKUS

Pause. Then jumps excitedly, applauding.

---

[4] **You chop, me chop; palaver finish.** Literally, "you eat and I eat also; that ends all the talk." It means, "I must get my share of the bribes which you receive."

[5] **I put for them.** "I bribed them."

That's what they say here? "Wusai den tie goat na dey e dey eat?" A tied goat that doesn't eat the grass around it is one dead goat.

> *Abass nods, Joshua laughs, and Brukus, pleaded with his defense, Dusts off his helmet.*

ABASS
In a tearful voice.
Joshua, our country is dying...
Long pause.

JOSHUA
Clears his throat, and takes a deep breath.
Abass, it's not only the poor, the uneducated that are dying, but also the men of learning: today, our society has produced two different species—Man and Lion. We are locked in a cage where the strong become more powerful and rich, and the weak forever poor and insecure.

ABASS
Bewildered; after a long thought.
Desperation is the womb of mischief! The world I saw at the mental hospital was deathly and sickly, but it is not only the clinically insane ones that need cure, but all of us—you and I, and people like Brukus who only chop when the other chops.

BRUKUS
Man, I don't see anything wrong in that. This is the way things are here—and if you think I'm wrong, wait, and you'll see—but I don't think our country is dying. If you want to be happy, you can be happy.

JOSHUA

You can be happy, but how about the others? Are they also happy?

BRUKUS

After a long pause.

Why not? Most of them are married. Just get yourself a beautiful wife, children, a car, and palaver finish. I know Abass will soon get himself a beautiful wife; all his problems will be solved.

ABASS

Who, me?

BRUKUS

Yes, you! Get a wife. Except if you want to be Old-Papa-Young-Boy.[6] Like all of these Senior Service—"these my cars!"

JOSHUA

Suddenly.

Ho, my upper lip trembles.

BRUKUS

With sharp severity.

Beware of getting in a quarrel...So Fatimah will marry Saidu next week.

ABASS

Yes, that's what Father has decided.

---

[6] **Old—papa-young boy.** An unscrupulous old man who sexually pursues young women.

BRUKUS

Good God! What will Saidu do with such a beautiful young girl? Won't the girl be unhappy?

JOSHUA

Why, do you want her? Do you want to marry six women, with all your education? Of course, you are not a university graduate.

BRUKUS
A little irritated.
I don't expect you to talk like that.

JOSHUA

Oh, the palm of my right hand itches.

BRUKUS
Severely, nodding earnestly.
Look forward to getting some money.

JOSHUA
Laughing.
Who'd give me money?

ABASS

I'd wanted to ask Pastor Brown about one strange dream I had when I was in London. This happened on a Saturday, the night before I left London. I dreamed I had lost my back teeth, my molars.

BRUKUS
Jumping.
Death! It means death, of a very close relative.
Quickly takes off his helmet and sticks a finger in his mouth, then wipes his face. Earnestly.
It happened with me once. That's a bad dream. If it were the front teeth, it could have been a friend or a distant relation—but the back teeth... Hmm-mm-mm.
Shakes his head violently. Joshua and Abass laugh aloud and long.

ABASS
Brukus! You are really funny. Not that I lost my teeth, it was my back teeth, the molars. And when I got up, I went to the looking glass and, shockingly, I hadn't lost a tooth. I burned the bed sheet and pillowcase I slept on. I was terribly disturbed. I don't believe in senseless dreams anymore, not since I've been to London. But here in Africa, one is tempted to believe. Even though it was a dream, I couldn't smile the whole day. When my sweetheart asked me, I said I had been to the dentist.
All laugh.

BRUKUS
Of course, Abass: you should believe in dreams like those. You were born and raised in Africa.

JOSHUA
With contempt.
Man, that was just a dream.

BRUKUS

Holding up his spread hand.

Don't say that!

Softly.

It's not just a dream. If I were you, Abass, I would tell my mother.

ABASS

Oh, come on, Brukus; you always misinterpret things. What bothered me at that time was how I could have met my sweetheart with most of my teeth missing.

BRUKUS

Earnestly.

Abass, I had a dream of that sort two years ago. Two weeks later I lost my father. You see, a dream is a dream, but through noting the recurrence of similar experiences, one will always interpret things correctly. It's a bad dream. It means you will lose your dearest relatives.

Joshua and Abass laugh.

I've never been overseas, but I know much about our customs. What does Sigmund Freud know about dreams and their African interpretations? Freud is a fraud, when it comes to African dreams.

JOSHUA

Freud? That man knew more about dreams, and was also more potent than you, sexually, I mean? Well, since you are Joseph the dreamer, how will you interpret this event, Brukus? This is a strange event that still baffles me. It's a strange thing I saw last week.

BRUKUS

Ready to seize the opportunity.

What is it?

JOSHUA

It is about a woman who died in our neighborhood. Some of the neighbors accused her of witchery. Since the time I moved to that neighborhood, infants have been dying every day. This woman who the others called a witch died last Saturday.

BRUKUS

Holding his chin and shaking his head.

What a bad day she chose to die. Mark it, it's a bad sign. Anything that happens with you on a Saturday, whether it's fortune or ill luck, will repeat itself three times. Two more people will die in that neighborhood.

ABASS

Shocked.

Is that so?

JOSHUA

The corpse of this woman refused to go to the grave. The coffin-bearers were rooted to their feet. They had to call a witch doctor before it finally moved to the cemetery. Even then it was a slow procession.

ABASS

Nonsense! You, an educated man, Joshua. Nonsense! What power does a dead man have over us? Nonsense!

BRUKUS
Don't deny that, Abass.

ABASS
How come I never saw a ghost while I was overseas? In France, I almost slept in a cemetery. French people bury their dead in their cities, towns and backyards. They don't dread the dead as evil spirits. Cemeteries overseas look like our parks here. I never did see a ghost while I was in London, or America. What is the difference between dead bodies? Why do we regard Joshua's dead body good and Brukus's dead body evil?

BRUKUS
Angered.
Don't say that. Not my dead body. I will be a good dead boy once I retire from this job. But don't deny that, Abass—

JOSHUA
I don't quite believe, but I saw it with my own eyes. The dead body refused to go to the cemetery.

ABASS
Sharply, rising.
Why didn't they give it a good punch in the head or put some hot iron rod across its backside?
All laugh.
Sure, if a dead body refused to go to the grave, the only way to make it run like a jet plane is to put a hot iron across its—

BRUKUS
Interrupting. In a tearful voice; softly.

Abass, that wouldn't be a nice thing to do. The dead body of the woman refused to move because it feared what it saw in her grave: the heap of dust and the angel of fire that awaits her.

ABASS

Oh, Brukus, your ideas will frighten infants from being born because you see nothing good in life and death. I know it is possible to see a ghost and have queer dreams in Africa. People here all have queer ideas, strange dreams, imagination and that nonsense.

Fatimah enters, bows before Abass.

FATIMAH

Courteously.

Brother, the food is ready.

ABASS

To the rest.

Well, gentlemen, let's go and eat. Forget about ghosts, and dead bodies that refuse to go to the grave. Nonsense.

They all go into Nene's mud house. A drum rolls.

BLACK OUT

Scene Three

Two weeks later. The night prior to the wedding ceremony. This scene can be done at center stage, in the space that serves as the compound. It opens in an old cemetery. Before us is a new grave, that of Makalay, about two months old. To the left of the grave are two buckets. The larger one is half full of water. The smaller bucket contains roots, herbs and medicinal leaves; it is covered with a piece of white satin. Tied to the bucket that contains the medicinal herbs is a red chicken. Lying next to it are a bundle of clothes and pieces of white, red, and black satin. Next to it is a wooden bowl that contains flour mixed with water. To the right of the grave are a low stool and a small wooden bowl of unhulled rice. As the stage lights brighten, Nene and Fatimah enter stage right. Nene is simply dressed in a thin white gown with a dark veil over her head. Fatimah wears only a loincloth and a head tie around her breasts. As they reach the center of the cemetery, a drum rolls then thunder and lightning.

> *Nene draws Fatimah closer to her. They both take off their sandals and quietly bow before the grave.*

NENE
Taking off her veil and rising, to Fatimah.
This is not the first time I have brought you here. I bring you here to cleanse you of the filth Drissa and Baimbadi did to your body. Remember that I'm here to help you. I will not help you if you refuse to tell the truth. I know you are an innocent and honest child.
Pointing to the grave.
The one that lies here was your foster mother. She was the

one who took you by the hand and led you into the Bondo bush. As a woman, you know how much that means to us. I know you are no longer a virgin because you've been ravished. Why I'm insisting on celebrating this custom is to help you reveal to us in public those that had ravished you. You know them, don't you?

> FATIMAH
> *Still kneeling before the grave.*

Yes, Auntie.

> NENE

I know you won't dare say it before their eyes because of the powerful charms they made you drink. Look, I brought you here to put darkness between them and you. I brought you here to throw cold water upon your body and on your foster mother's grave. I brought you here to wash your guts of the charms Drissa and Baimbadi made you drink. Remember, the one that lies here was my twin sister. I have my supernatural power, and will do everything to help you. The bush that your enemies plant in your backyard will provide the ropes to tie them hand and foot. You want your life, don't you?

> FATIMAH
> *Still kneeling before the grave, trembling.*

Auntie, I want my life. I want to live.
> *Almost crying.*

I don't want to die young. I... I will speak tomorrow.

> NENE
> *Pleased.*

Good, then. Since you've promised to speak tomorrow, I'll do all I can to help you. I need not say more. I cannot go before the elders and tell them what I know. You have the right to speak out tomorrow because they will ask you who did this or that to you if they find out you are not a virgin. I'm helpless, child. A woman is a woman. I depend on you.

A slight pause. Wipes a tear.

Rise up and pass me the bundle.

Fatimah does so. Nene undoes it and unties a small bundle containing rice powder. She goes before the grave, kneels, holding the rice powder and moving her lips. Slowly rises and then scatters the rice powder on the grave. Goes around the grave five times.

To Fatimah.

Bring me the wooden stool.

Fatimah does so. Nene puts the stool on the grave. From the bundle, she takes the red satin and covers the stool and the whole grave.

Come and sit on the stool.

Fatimah does so, trembling.

FATIMAH

Auntie, I'm feeling cold.

NENE

Severely.

Stay there! Don't move.

Nene returns to the grave with the bowl that contains the white flour mixed with water. Stands behind Fatimah and, moving her lips, keeps rubbing her head with her right hand. With the mixture she makes several dots on

*Fatimah's back, then a cross on her stomach, then one on
the toes of each foot. She returns the bowl and takes the
one full of rice; pours some rice grains on Fatimah's head;
gets the chicken and returns to the grave. Stands behind
Fatimah, facing the audience, and holds the chicken in
the air, moving her lips. Then holds the chicken closer to
Fatimah's head.*

Makalay, I have brought you your adopted child, Fatimah.
Tomorrow is her wedding day and I have asked her to reveal
the whole secret on that day. I want her to name publicly
those who raped her, those who killed you and your daughter. Baimbadi and Drissa gave her powerful charms that
would destroy her if the child decided to speak out. I don't
want your shadow to frighten her anymore. Fatimah dares
not enter your room even at daytime. She is afraid of your
shadow. I want you to help us.

    Holds the chicken high and shouts.

And you, my dead Pasorie, Pamorah, Yakhaku, Pabomenah,
and all our dead ancestors, hear this case. If this our common
child, Fatimah, decides to live by daring to talk, let this cockerel peck the rice off her head.

    *Nene lowers the chicken to peck the rice off Fatimah's
head. The chicken does not move. She tries again; the
chicken responds but it is not a very auspicious result.
Nene shakes her head violently, but says nothing. Then,
to Fatimah.*

Here, hold the chicken and don't move.

    *Fatimah does so. Nene takes pieces of the white and
black satin from the bundle. Covers Fatimah with the
black satin and then with the white satin. She puts her
hands on her head, moving her lips.*

The lights slowly dim.

Pray quietly to yourself. Curse those that had almost ruined your life to die like vultures and rot like this chicken. Pray for all the good things you need in life.

> *As the stage lights brighten, Nene is seen standing behind Fatimah. She begins to uncover her. She collects dust from the grave, pours water from the bucket that contains the medicinal herbs, and returns to the grave.*

This mixture will kill everything poisonous in your stomach. But remember, if you fail to talk, it will also destroy you. I'll drink it first.

> *She does so and then hands the bowl to Fatimah, who hesitates.*

Drink it, witch!

> *Fatimah does so, her whole body shaking.*

FATIMAH

Auntie, will you save my life?

NENE

It's not me who will save you. It is yourself. If you continue to conceal what you know about my sister's death, you'll die unmarried, with a swollen stomach and with broken arms and legs. This chicken, I will pluck all its feathers and pierce it with needles before I dump it into the bush where children defecate. You will rot in that way if you fail to speak tomorrow.

> *Collects dust from the grave and puts it into a bundle.*

I will scatter this dust in the compound. Everyone who steps on it and knows the cause of my sister's death but has refused to bring it to light will die.

> *To Fatimah.*

Rise and kneel with me before this grave.

> *They kneel. Then they rise. Nene, holding a short broom,
> and Fatimah, holding the tail end of her lapa, go round
> the grave seven times. On each round, Nene recites a
> curse in Temne: "Mein terr kor, en terr entoko kor mu."[7]
> Fatimah repeats it after her. Then they stop.*

NENE
To Fatimah.
Give me the chicken. Go to the river and dump these things.
Don't turn to look back. Come home at once. Wash yourself
clean and then come home. I'll be with you soon.

> *Nene collects the two buckets, the bundles, the stool, the
> chicken, and some other things. She leaves the cemetery
> and exits backwards. A slight pause, then thunder and
> lightning. Fatimah collects the remaining things and be-
> gins to leave, walking backwards. Baimbadi enters, car-
> rying a bowl of kola nuts pierced with needles. Fatimah,
> walking backwards, collides with Baimbadi and screams;
> sees Baimbadi and trembles.*

BAIMBADI
Oh! What is the matter with you? Where are you coming
from so late at night?

> *Fatimah does not answer.*

Here, drink this quickly. I brought you this mixture with some
kola nuts. Drink it quickly. This will help you tomorrow. I'll
cut your fingers and ears if you don't drink it.

> *Fatimah hesitantly does so.*

---

[7] **Mein terr ko... kor mu.** "If you the ancestors let this crime go unpunished,
then you must not accept this sacrificial chicken, but let it go free."

Here, chew this kola.

> *Fatimah continues to tremble. Nene is heard offstage.*
> *Baimbadi quickly leaves stage left. Nene enters stage*
> *right. Runs quickly to Fatimah.*

NENE

What is the matter?

> *Fatimah doe not answer. She burst into tears.*

BLACK OUT

Act Three

Africa has always died to the rhythm of its own dance and song and laughter.

— Ezekiel Mphahlele, *The Wanderers*

Scene One

The following day. It is now 4 p.m. The lights on the stage rise to a brilliant intensity. Before us is Chief Drissa's compound. Chairs and benches are arranged in a semicircle. Offstage, the women are singing a familiar wedding song, accompanied by faint drumming and the sound of the balangi.[1]

Pabuya, the market sweeper, enters stage left. He is smartly dressed but his gabardine trousers are too big. His long shirt is worn out. His head is shaved and he holds a hat cocked against his left shoulder. A whistle hangs around his neck. He staggers onto the stage, dead drunk. There is a large omole[2] bottle in one of his back pockets. He walks toward center stage and scrutinizes the chairs and benches; takes his bottle, drinks a little, and belches; holds the bottle in the air and bursts out singing "The Song of Love and the World."

PABUYA
Dhu-ru duhponduhsu. Sa la yi!
Tay mee law maw bawthee.
Wawyow!
Muhn te ta-ta-ta-to long,
Tay mee law maw bawthee.
> *Laughs as he pours libation. Shaking the bottle earnestly.*
For all them dead people. Dis na great day en' we invite wun-na all for cam. All them neighba' them.
> *He waves with his hat to an imaginary crowd. Then he begins to sing and dance quietly.*
Eebee-eebee-eebee yay!

---

[1] **Balangi.** A wooden xylophone.
[2] **Omole.** A very strong palm wine liquor.

Yawo, mamee, ay bee saw!
Yawo, mamee, ay bee saw!
> *Stops and smiles.*

Happy Christmas! Happy Christmas me nor die!
> *As he wipes his mouth with his back hand, footsteps are heard. He quickly sits down on the wooden bench. Abass, Brukus and Joshua enter, dressed in traditional costumes, except for Joshua, who is in his Sunday suit.*

PABUYA
Pss! Wudat look yawoh na in eye na in know say Yawoh dey cry.[3]

BRUKUS
Pleased at seeing Pabuya.
See! See! Pabuya is here already. What a surprise!

PABUYA
Rising and beaming. Excitedly.
Well, me no dey for bachelor 'eve; so me can the wedding now. Me can for cheer the yawoh.[4]

ABASS
Well, be our guest.
> *They all sit on the wooden bench.*

PABUYA
To Abass.

---
[3] **Psss! Wudat... dey cry.** "Hey! Who looks the bride in the eye knows that the bride does cry."
[4] **Well, me no dey...yawoh.** "Well, I wasn't there for the bachelor party, so I've come to the wedding to cheer the bride."

Mas'er! Why you nor sit yanda. Them chair yanda them look fine.

> *Drinks, gaps, and the rest laugh.*

ABASS

No, Pabuya. I'll sit with you all. You know, Joshua, I bitterly opposed this ceremony.

JOSHUA
Shocked.

Why?

ABASS

I don't think this custom serves its purpose anymore.
> *Long pause.*

I think we are only celebrating such custom for the fun of it and not for what it holds. I don't believe in it anymore. How many more virgins are there left among our young women... Was your (pause)... a virgin?

BRUKUS
Not listening.

What! Abass, are you dreaming? Don't you know the purpose of marrying a virgin girl?

ABASS

Only a damn fool will believe that Fatimah is still a virgin. You can tell a ripe corn by its look. Don't you see her breasts?

BRUKUS
Rises and says defensively.

Abass, you know nothing about women. I have four wives and I'm only thirty-five. Each one of them respects, honors and fears me. Do you know why? Because I was the first man to see beyond their lapa.[5] And they were all virgins. I will damn myself if I marry a woman that's not a virgin. God forbid! Fen-fen-fen![6] Not man Brukus!

Sits heavily on the wooden bench. The rest laugh.

PABUYA

Me nor get wife but me know watin dis man they talk. But them pikin them dis days, them like tolon-tolon[7] pass anything. How you go get virgin them days. Pikin want ashobi,[8] them want pon-pon-peep![9] Them want miniskirt, them want money.

Drinks.

So, them man' self go do them yone.

Shaking his head violently.

Woman don' lost in respect. Man see woman now like omolanke[10] wagon. Them push 'am forward, 'e go forward; them push'an behen', in go behen'.

Turns sharply to Brukus. Shouting.

You get the liber? You get the lee?[11] You get car? You na minister?

---

[5] **The first man to see beyond their lapa.** A lapa is a woman's loincloth; hence, this is an image of defloration.

[6] **Fen-fen-fen.** "Never-never-never."

[7] **Tolon-tolon.** Literally, "phallus-phallus." He is saying that the young women are sexually very desirous.

[8] **Ashobi.** Fancy dress worn on festive occasions.

[9] **Pon-pon-peep.** The sound of an automobile horn; hence, an automobile.

[10] **Omolanke.** A two-wheeled pushcart for carrying heavy loads.

[11] **Liber, lee.** Equivalent slang terms corresponding to the American "guts." Both derive from the word "liver."

Pabuya laughs long and loud. Then to Abass and Joshua.
Master, Worl' don' poil.[12] Worl' do for fraid!
Long pause. He drinks, shaking his head.

JOSHUA
To Abass, while Brukus contemptuously stares at Pabuya.
He's right. We push our women like Omolanke. They only go
where we need them to be.

ABASS
Cutting in.
That's right. It's a dog's life. Even a broken canoe is useful
sometimes.

PABUYA
Rises. Singing and dancing.
"Broko canoo nar bay get' in owner. Make we lef'am so" cause
e want' am so!
Eebee-eebee yay!
*On Pabuya's last line, the women offstage chant the line,
"Eebee-eebee yay!"*

JOSHUA
I think they are coming now.
Let's sit down and wait.
*They sit. Stage left, a crowd of women enters and pro-
ceeds towards the stage front. They are dressed in tradi-
tional costumes. Leading the procession is a young woman
dressed in white and carrying a calabash on her head.
About her is a group of young women who hold a piece of*

---

[12] **Worl'don'poil.** "The world has been irrevocably spoiled."

*white satin above her head. Also under this white cloth is
Fatimah. Her hair is beautifully plaited and around her
waist is a string of colorful beads. She wears a Yarasha[13]
that reaches her ankles. Dancing in front of Fatimah is
the GODMAMY, the overseer of the tribal marriage
ceremonies. She is tall, rugged, and rough; her bearded
face is painted with charcoal ashes. She wears men's
clothes: a sultan cap,[14] a big, voluminous dark boubou,
and old, worn-out shoes that show her toes. A protruding
scrotum hangs loose between her legs, and she walks with
a scissoring motion, one foot in front of the other, as if
the scrotum were painful. She carries a staff whose top is
a mask. In the procession are Baimbadi, Pastor Brown,
Saidu and Nene, all dressed in Traditional costumes. The
crowd sings as it moves.*

GODMAMY
Ee-Ma Yelli-oh!

CROWD
Ee-Ma yeli te-te!

GODMAMY
Ee-Ma yeli-bah!

CROWD
Ee-Ma yeli te-te!

---

[13] **Yarasha.** A woman's skirt. The cloth is cut, full-length, into very narrow
strips.
[14] **Sultan cap.** A cylindrical cap, two to twelve inches tall.

GODMAMY

Eebee-eebee yay!

Pabuya joins the crowd and they all dance; then the crowd sits on the wooden benches and the family sits in the chairs. The Godmamy comes forward.

GODMAMY

We gather here to celebrate custom, and honor Saidu and Fatimah: the groom and the bride. We the women also salute everyone that's here with us.

The women confer among themselves; then,

Give me the calabash.

The woman with the calabash does so.

Inside this calabash are a whole piece of satin; a knot of white thread; needles, and the dowry. On behalf of the Bangura family, we are asked to present this calabash to the crowd.

BRUKUS

Interrupting.

How much is the dowry?

PASTOR BROWN

To Brukus, sharply.

This is a religious gathering, Mister! If you can't behave...

Indicating with disgust.

there is the door!

BRUKUS

A little irritated.

To hell with that, Pastor. I am thirty-five, and have four women and five children. What about you? Don't tell me—

PASTOR BROWN
Shhh! Don't!

GODMAMY
I will fine both of you if you interrupt this meeting. So as I was saying: I hope God will make these two husband and wife.
> *She hands the calabash to Nene, Nene hands it to Baimbadi, and Baimbadi hands it to Pastor Brown, who puts the calabash in the center.*

PASTOR BROWN
> *Holding his Bible aloft and kissing it.*

May good angels put their hands on this calabash. "Jesus, Son of God, and Virgin Mary, Mother of Christ." Amen.
> *He sits down heavily. Abass, Joshua, and Brukus laugh.*

GODMAMY
> *Comes forward.*

May I ask Saidu and Fatimah to come forward.
> *Both come forward. Saidu stands on the left and Fatimah on the right, facing the audience. The calabash stands before them. To Saidu.*

Saidu, if you agree to this family marriage, take the calabash on the ground, and give it to Fatimah.
> *Saidu takes it and gives it to Fatimah.*

SAIDU
> *To Fatimah and the rest.*

If Fatimah agrees to become my wife, let her take the calabash from the ground.
> *He puts the calabash on the ground.*

GODMAMY
To Fatimah.

Take it if you agree to become his wife.

> *Fatimah turns around, stares sternly at Nene, drops her head, and begins to dig the ground with her foot.*

BAIMBADI
Angrily.

You dead fish take it and don't keep turning around. We don't have time to waste.

ABASS
To Baimbadi.

I don't think it's fair to frighten her. Let her decide what she thinks is best for her.

PASTOR BROWN
To Abass.

Dady Joe![15] It would be better if you remained quiet.

> *To Fatimah.*

Woman, if you love Saidu, take it.

NENE
Impatiently.

What are you waiting for?

> *Fatimah bows and takes the calabash. Rises, faces the Godmamy, bows gently and hands her the calabash.*

CROWD
With some excitement.

---

[15] **Dady Joe.** Roughly equivalent to American "hey, buddy."

Eebee-eebee yay!

The crowd settles down again.

GODMAMY
To Saidu and Fatimah.

Since you've decided to become husband and wife, now follow me into that room.

*They leave, heading for Saidu's room behind the yard,
followed by some women. They exit stage left.*

ABASS
Displeased and embarrassed; emphatically.

The whole thing is senseless!

BAIMBADI
Rises, furiously; to Abass.

Senseless! Now look here, if you have no respect for custom,
go out and become Opotho! That's what you want to be:
Opotho, a white man!

PASTOR BROWN

Opotho! Say opothai—when something is rotten, they say
opothai.

Pabuya laughs rudely.

ABASS

Opotho or opothai, call me white man or what you will. But
it's senseless.

NENE
To Abass.

My son, don't say that. We all started this way. Wait for the women.

> *Abass sits harshly, Joshua and Brukus whistle, and Pabuya chuckles. The women return; Fatimah now wears a long red boubou. Rises and anxiously says.*

What did you find? Is she a virgin?

BAIMADI
Sharply to Nene, interrupting.
Be patient, woman. The women don't hide anything.

NENE
Sitting down.
I hope so.

GODMAMY
I want to ask Fatimah a few questions. When the kabap bird chirps, you listen to its cries before you say this or that. Fatimah, did you know Saidu as man before he declared to marry you?

FATIMAH
Softly.
No, I didn't.

GODMAMY
You didn't! Did any other man touch you before? I mean, who first saw beyond your lapa?

> *Fatimah doesn't answer.*

NENE

Won't you answer the question?

BAIMBADI

No, no, we will not have it. She will answer only to that woman.

GODMAMY

Fatimah, how many men have gone to bed with you, apart from Saidu?

FATIMAH

Digging the ground, speaking through her teeth.

I don't know.

Pause.

I... I...

Speechless.

GODMAMY

To Saidu.

Saidu, did you ever touch Fatimah as a wife before?

SAIDU

No; I have never known her as a wife. I am innocent today.

All laugh.

You can ask Father. He can tell you.

ABASS

He is both angry and about to laugh.

So you were a virgin all those years!

109

JOSHUA
What a saint!

PASTOR BROWN
He's a saint indeed, unlike you.
> *Pause. Nene comes forward. Angrily she strips of both her own gown and lapa and Fatimah's as well, so that they are clad only in their short underskirts, their waist beads exposed. She takes off her head tie and ties it around her waist, gathers the tail end of her lapa and stamps once, then spits on Fatimah's lapa as it lies on the ground. She picks up Fatimah's head tie and fastens it around her own waist; takes the calabash, puts it between her legs, and stands astride it. Baimbadi stands, furious and shocked at her behavior. The rest stand in amazement.*

NENE
> *To the Godmamy, angrily.*
Ask her again.

BAIMBADI
> *Sharply to Nene.*
Will you get back to your seat!

NENE
I! Not until I see my grave. This child will speak! She will tell us who is responsible for this shameful act. Much blood has been shed in this house. No, I will not sit, and don't dare tell me that. I am a woman, and I cannot sit here and watch womanhood disgraced and ridiculed. Husband and wife are like nail in bench. But today, even Allah or God will hear me

if I deny your voice, Baimba.

> *Shouting, to Fatimah and the Godmamy.*

Come here, witch!

> *Pulls Fatimah by the ear; to the Godmamy.*

Ask her again. Ask her!

> *Puts the calabash between her legs, and claps her hands in front of Fatimah's face.*

ABASS
Rising.
The child is not a virgin! Why don't we say it?

NENE
To Fatimah.
Are you a virgin, Fatimah?

BAIMBADI
Sharply to Nene.
Are you taking over this place?

NENE
Ignores him.
Fatimah, remember well who is responsible for this shameful act!

> *Fatimah abruptly convulses, shaking nervously.*

FATIMAH
Holding her head with her hands.
"Let's do it," he tells me every night.

NENE

Who? Who? Who asked you to do it?

Baimbadi rises, but Pastor Brown restrains him; he sits down again.

FATIMAH

Kriffi. The kriffi!

Nene, shocked and in bewildered anger, spits in Fatimah's face. The young women dancers abruptly exit. Everyone is stunned. A long pause. Nene holds her chin, exhausted, and keeps staring at Fatimah.

GODMAMY

Coming forward.

Do it! Do what?

FATIMAH

In a terrified voice.

He says, "Now you are my wife, I'll take you to the mountains and rivers and cut your fingers and ears."

GODMAMY

To Fatimah.

Did you sleep with this kriffi?

FATIMAH

Yes, yes... He puts it in me and takes my blood away. He'd kill me if I refused.

GODMAMY

Kill you! What's his name?

FATIMAH
Weeps, and says quickly.

Banni!

Pauses. All stares piercingly at her.

GODMAMY
Banni! The devil of the Great Scarcies River.

PASTOR BROWN
Bewildered, almost speechless; rising.

This child has sold her soul to the devil!

FATIMAH
In a state of convulsion.

Baim-Baim- Driss-Driss—

Breaks off in tears. Then bursts out with uncontrolled anger, and helplessness.

Ban-ban, dirr! Dirr! Ban-banni! Banie! Ban-ban-ban-ban-ban.

NENE
Grabs Fatimah by the ear, almost shouting in her face.

And I'll whip the kriffi out of you. Look here, since this is the way you want to end, your Banni and your kriffis will keep you in a cigarette tin!

Nene exits, dragging Fatimah by the ear. They all leave except Pabuya, Baimbadi, and the Godmamy, who picks up the clothes and some of the paraphernalia, stares piercingly at Baimbadi, and exits. The lights become bright. Baimbadi and Pabuya are left at the center stage. A long and awkward silence. Pabuya keeps staring at Baimbadi

113

and shaking his head. Spits, almost in Baimbadi's face, and then bursts out laughing. Points a finger at him and shouts.

PABUYA
Kriffi? Na devil pikin!

BLACK OUT

Scene Two

Hours later. Outside Chief Drissa's compound. The scene opens quietly. As the stage lights brighten, Baimbadi, now in a dark gown, is seen walking back and forth, very nervous. Abass sits beside Pastor Brown, who is still in his old Sunday suit.

PASTOR BROWN
Takes a deep breath. To Abass.
My child, I'm a Christian, but that is one thing we find impossible for our Christian natives to give up: The Bondo Society. In the old days, the punishment for a woman who was not a virgin was terrible. They would cut off parts of her ears and fingers before the husband would accept her as his bed partner. They have a reason for it, my son. For them, it strengthens fidelity, love and marriage.

ABASS
Pastor, that was in the past, not today...

BAIMBADI
Angrily to Abass.
To hell with today! That girl deserves to be locked up with chickens and goats in the same room.
Pause.
If it were not for the law—

ABASS
Is there no other thing in life Fatimah could accomplish? Must we treat her like a slave?

BAIMBADI

Slave! Slave! Yes, she is a slave—she's fit to be one. She is one already...

ABASS

Becoming irritated.

If she is one, then who is responsible for what she is now? Who has made her a slave? If you and your brother had not sacrificed this family to something that's dying ... You believe in political power and chieftaincy—but that's a dead institution. It's dying, Father. No one believes in chieftaincy anymore. If you had loved this family, you and your brother, Drissa, would have saved the family. But see what is happening to it—

BAIMBADI

What is happening to it? What are you talking about? Look here, if I never cared for the family, you could have been a carpenter or a bricklayer right now. But I paid all my money to educate you. And now you need not thank me—I am the black devil here. This is what Nene is telling you. Yes, I know that...

Long pause. Very thoughtful.

But my son, you cannot fish in a desert. I was warned in a dream that my brother Drissa would be crowned chief of Kissy if we fought for the crown. I believed in it. I believed that it was only Drissa who was capable of helping this town. Everyone was happy when my brother became chief. My son, a child born today will not walk tomorrow. I need not go in the street, and put my hands on top of my head and go weeping like a woman... Hmm? God knows that I care. But your mother doesn't trust me; doesn't trust anyone, because of her sister's death…

PASTOR BROWN

When the tallest tree in the bush falls, all the little ones wither away. If our Lord Christ died on the cross for our sins, who else will not die?

Pause.

We too will die someday.

BAIMBADI

Sits beside Abass and gives him his hand.

Abass, I'm still your father. Shake hands with me.

Takes his hand, but Abass doesn't respond.

Abass, will you shake my hand? My son, one does not run where one is expected to walk.

Rises, disappointed.

Well, if you only respect your mother, you are not helping the family. Nene knows that I am the man here. A woman must respect her husband and listen to him. But your mother—

PASTOR BROWN

Foolishly interrupting.

The place of a woman is in the home, with her husband and children.

ABASS

Rising; to Pastor Brown, angrily, then ironically.

Oh really! Pastor: people must grow out of things that have outlived their usefulness! You still think a woman is like the tail of a cow and must follow her husband even if he is a dead goat.

117

BAIMBADI
Angrily.

I, a goat? You hear that, Pastor?

PASTOR BROWN
Jokingly.

Now sit down! He is your father and I am still your teacher. If you don't, I'll whip you.

Looks around for a whip.

Where is the whip? I'll whip him! I'll use my belt if you don't sit down. Now sit!

Abass sits down heavily. Pastor Brown shakes his finger at him.

I don't want to hear anything from you.

To Baimbadi.

You sit down too, Baimbadi.

BAIMBADI
Still standing.

To listen to a donkey! He calls me a goat!

ABASS

To hell with that! I was only giving an example.

BAIMBADI
Angrily.

Don't make an example of me. I am not a plum that children play with.

PASTOR BROWN
To Abass.

Child, you are lost.

ABASS
Rising angrily, to both Pastor and Baimbadi.
Lost! Who is lost? I don't think both of you are in your proper frame of mind. Do you know how much has gone from our family? Do you? Why do you have children? Are we born only to suffer? See what has become of my mother, Nene. Where is Auntie Makalay? Where is my niece Abbi? Where are they? See what has happened to your first-born, Saidu: Saidu is now forty, and he's still buried in this dark place. Saidu does nothing but feed sparrows, beat the tabule, talk about bygone days or tell stupid stories to women. What have you given to him—life? This is the way you two want us to be, like Saidu. He is just like the rest of them: they get up at sunrise; watch the sunset and go to sleep; pray thirty times a day. There is nothing to do. Nothing. Not because they are lazy—you simply have not taught them how to live. They have no dreams of their own, and you have not given them any. In a few more years you will leave us nothing but open graves and shrouds to bury ourselves, or else sacrifice us like chickens—

PASTOR BROWN
Sacrifice! The world has gone mad!

BAIMBADI
This world is coming to an end.

ABASS
Yes. You are making it so.
To Pastor Brown.

Pastor, I see religion is mixed with tradition. Man's word becomes God's word—we are all mad, aren't we? Then I say God is dead!

PASTOR BROWN
Angrily; rises and shakes a finger at Abass.
I don't preach custom! I don't mix God's word with man's word! I preach the Bible! I'm a proper Christian.

ABASS
With uncontrolled anger.
Then stop sleeping, Pastor. Both of you! Open your eyes! Suffering is not a Holy Communion—it takes you nowhere, Pastor. Let the people live! But you two would prefer to suffer and live in misery, as long as there is a heaven. But one must die before one goes to heaven. Which do you prefer, heaven or earth? We can't hold on to falling trees anymore...
Saidu enters, carrying a bundle. Long pause.

SAIDU
Perplexed; through tears.
Uncle, Uncle... Uncle Drissa is dying.
Pause.
The doctors asked me to bring his clothes.
Gives the bundle to Baimbadi, who is now trembling.

PASTOR BROWN
Turns to Abass.
Abass! What must we do?

ABASS
Through tears.
Uncle Drissa is dying?
Offstage, Fatimah is singing. They listen. Pause.
Who is singing?
They all stand, listening.

SAIDU
Fatimah is singing a song of death.
He breaks off, sobbing. Abass begins to comfort him. As the lights fade out on them, Fatimah is seen coming to stage front, at left. She is naked to the waist, her arms clasped on her breasts. She walks quietly, singing through tears, singing "The Song of the Beautiful Young Girl Who Dies Unmarried."

FATIMAH
Meene bawkye saw,
Bokye tee kuh-bala,
Oh! Yenken.
Awrong duh Muhyehfa,
Deh feer uhl' p-aw,
Unlup eh-Sehwe, ay! Yenken.
Pause.
...And then she died.
She walks backwards, leaving stage left. The lights again begin to glow on the compound. Pastor Brown, Saidu, and Abass descend, and quietly disappear behind the stage.

BAIMBADI
Lost in thought.

The hospital has killed Drissa...

> *He comes down to center stage. The lights on Nene's room brighten. Nene is heard talking to herself. Baimbadi, unseen, quietly comes in and stands in the doorway, watching and listening.*

NENE
With her back towards Baimbadi.

Trust no one, Abass. I have told you. There are deep holes in this compound. You'll see them if you have eyes.

BAIMBADI
Calmly enters; both keep staring at each other.

So this is what you've been telling your son. Not to trust anyone.

NENE
Determined to face him.

Do you trust anyone?

BAIMBADI
Still controlled.

Nene, you are putting yourself between Abass and me. You are not helping the family...

> *Pause; sees the pictures covered.*

Are you still talking to the dead, Nene? Why do you do it? It is a great sin against Allah. You know that. Now I want you to uncover those pictures and turn them against the wall. You don't remember the dead that way. Nene, turn the pictures against the wall, wait for a while...

    Pause.

Drissa is dying. I have come to tell you that. Please stop frightening the children. The pictures frighten everyone...

NENE
Facing him, earnestly.

This is my room and those pictures will remain as they are.

BAIMBADI

But how can you live in here with the dead?

NENE

They are dead to you, but not to me. I will continue to mourn my sister's death. They don't frighten me...

    Baimbadi begins to shake.

Those pictures will remain as they are—

    Baimbadi reaches for the framed photo; pulls the picture from the wall; holds it in his hands, still shaking.

Destroy it! What else is there left that you've not done! Kill her a second time! Kill her!

    Baimbadi smashes the framed photo on the floor. Grabs the picture, tears it into pieces and scatters them on the floor. Both stand staring at each other. Then Nene, with mounting anger, spits on his face.

BAIMBADI
Calmly but with controlled anger says softly.

See what you've done. Why did you spit at me?

    Becoming openly angry again.

What else can you do? When I say sit, you sit. Your behavior is frightening everyone.

> *Nene puts her hands on top of her head, weeping. Before Baimbadi leaves, Nene kneels and picks up the torn pieces. Bows over them like a mother over the dead body of her only son. As Baimbadi leaves, she quickly picks up pieces of the picture and stands in the doorway.*

NENE

You think I'm only a woman, but you are wrong! You are a walking dead man...

> *The lights dim. She returns to her room. Sighing, through tears.*

Makalay, how will I see your face again?

> *Rises, picks up the bundle that contains the dust collected from the grave and puts it on the broken glass and the pieces of Makalay's picture. Energetically.*

Makalay! If the dead have power, avenge your death. Anyone that had a hand in your death or knows about your death but refuses to reveal it publicly must be destroyed as they step on this dust.

> *She goes to the compound and scatters the dust in all the corners of the compound. She leaves stage right. A few moments later, Fatimah enters stage left, carrying a bundle on her head. She puts the bundle down and quietly sits on it, staring into space.*

FATIMAH

After a long pause.

And this little girl comes to the center of the crossroads; and there she is trapped by a leopard. And then she sings a song to her mother to show her the right road that leads home.

Sings through tears.

Day mee woor'r-ay, kondo waima?

Awaima, waima, waima.

Pa Seepa, gbay!

Sawng mee rongay!

Awaima, waima, waima.

Wipes a tear.

But the dead mother never came; and when darkness came, the leopard fell on her and ate her. She died unmarried, and with no children and no grave. And no one remembers her ...Ah!

Rises furiously, speaking to imaginary people.

No! No! Stay where you are! I want no man to come near me. I'll go where there are only women.

Laughs bitterly, cynically.

And then, I'll live there forever!

Footsteps are heard. She grabs her bundle and hides her face in it. Saidu and Abass enter stage left. Saidu runs to Fatimah. Fatimah screams with all her breath.

ABASS

To Saidu.

Leave her alone! I'll take care of her.

Fatimah runs away from them.

FATIMAH

Drops the bundle.

Take it! Take it—now you have it!

She beats her breast and stamps her foot harshly on the ground.

125

Stay where you are! You see, there are holes in here.

Claps her arms, trembling, and shaking feverishly.

Oh, I am cold.

Screams and goes around in a circle.

Kill me! Kill me! Kill me! And they pierced the needles right into my heart.

Shaking, ready to collapse.

Now they have me. The kriffis! The needles...

Drops dead.

SAIDU

Shouting as he falls over her body, weeping.

No! Fatimah! Oh Fatu! Fatu! Fatu! You are my wife, Fatu.

ABASS

To Saidu.

I'll go and get an ambulance.

He runs off stage; then enter Pastor Brown, Brukus, and Joshua.

PASTOR BROWN

Shocked and bewildered, his knees knocking with fright, falls to his knees alongside Fatimah, clasping his Bible to his breasts.

What are you doing to her? Fatu! Fatu.

Shaking her.

Come, please, let's take her to the hospital.

They take Fatimah to the hospital, leaving stage right. Baimbadi enters stage left, talking to himself most of the time. He is barefoot and wears nothing except voluminous trousers. Then he walks quietly towards the bungalow and sits on the step, with bowed head. After a while, Pastor Brown, Joshua, Saidu, and Brukus enter, carrying Fatimah's body. Baimbadi slowly comes down the steps towards them. He covers his eyes with his hands and begins to weep.

BAIMABADI
Through tears.
Is she...is she dead, Pastor?

JOSHUA
The doctors at the hospital wanted to do a post mortem, but Pastor Brown wouldn't let them. She died an hour ago at the hospital.

BRUKUS
Abass and Nene are still at the hospital; they are trying to secure the dead body of Drissa.

BAIMBADI
Shaking his head.
Drissa is dead, and Fatimah also?

PASTOR BROWN
To Baimbadi.
Take up the body. Baimba, we will put the body behind the compound; you and I will go to the mortuary and claim Drissa's body. Take up the body.

The corpse bearers begin to move slowly. Suddenly they are halted by the bier that bears Fatimah's dead body.

They try to move, but the coffin is held back by some invisible and supernatural force.

PASTOR BROWN
Then to Baimbadi.
Baimba, the coffin bearing the dead body of Fatimah does not want to move. Come and stand before it. Perhaps the dead body of Fatimah will move. Please come down and stand before the coffin of Fatimah.

BAIMBADI
Almost in tears.
No, Pastor. I'm not a good man.

BRUKUS
Shouting.
This is calamity! This is calamity!

PASTOR BROWN
We will be here for days, Baimbadi. Come and stand before the corpse. You are her foster father. The body will not move if you don't stand before the coffin. Come down and lead the procession!

BAIMBADI
I will stand close by, but not stand before it.
They begin to move slowly, but are again halted. Baimbadi retreats; the corpse suddenly pushes the coffin ahead, forcing the carriers along with it, knocking Baimbadi to the ground. He groans like an animal being led to the slaughter.

PASTOR BROWN
Bewildered.
Put the body down! Put it down!
> *Everyone is confused. Pastor Brown kneels over Baim-badi. Enter Abass and Nene.*

ABASS
Running to the scene.
What is the matter? What is the matter?

BRUKUS
The dead body of Fatimah refused to move. Baimbadi was knocked dead by the coffin. All of a sudden, the coffin stops, forces us to turn round, and like a jet plane—Boom, and hits Baimbadi at his privates, I mean (*pauses*) that's what happened! The dead are at war with the living. Nothing but death and calamity. Hey! This na Wahala! Calamity! Pastor, Call upon God and Allah to come down and help. Your God cannot remain silent and indifferent anymore. Help!

ABASS
Nervous; turns to Nene.
What must we do, Nene?

NENE
Not wanting to speak.
Is he dead, Pastor?

PASTOR BROWN
I don't think he will live.
> *Abass and Saidu kneel over Baimbadi.*

He won't hear you anymore.

Nene takes one of her lapas and covers Baimbadi.

PASTOR BROWN

We must take both bodies behind the compound.

The bodies are taken offstage. The lights dim. Abass is still kneeling on the stage with his hands widely stretched up to the heavens. The lights brighten again.

ABASS

Shaking his head in despair.

Three dead bodies on the same day...

Softly.

"A child that crawls lives longer... Look closely under her ankles... Do her feet resemble those of human beings? Trust no one!" What is there in a cold dead body? What do I gain by looking at a dead body?

Pause.

Now I see it's not only the sick, the crippled, the blind and the mentally ill that need cure...Those who seem quite well are also deathly ill. I have returned to Africa, and I have been here only two weeks,... but each of my nerves is shaking. The shadow of death glares at me with a face of helplessness and despair... A broken spirit that's chained and caged in by falling walls—walls we can no longer mend. Walls that are crumbling down. What is there for us beyond those walls? Can I row backwards on a swift current that's running against me? No! We can't hold on to falling trees anymore. Now we must look beyond the withered trees for green ones. We must stand in the sun and do only that which is right and just. This is the only way...

Breaks off.

THE ONLY HOPE FROM THIS DEATH!

Nene enters with a bowl of water and moves her lips as she sprinkles the water at the spot where Baimbadi died, then all around the stage. Sets the bowl on the ground and stares at her son, who is still on his knees with his head buried in his hands, sobbing. She comes quietly and stands behind him. Seeing his mother, he struggles to stand. Nene helps him get on his feet, and he collapses in her arms. They hold each other weeping. Then the tabule is beaten three times: three hesitating beats that forebode death. The last beat is drowned by the wailing voices of women offstage. The lights slowly fade out.

THE END

Afterword

Afric Owns a Serpent[*]
by *Caldwell Titcomb*

The theatre of black Africa extends many centuries into the past. It has been predominantly a part of oral literature, closely allied with myth and ritual, and characterized by communal participation. Plays, in the European sense of fixed written texts performed by actors in front of passive audiences, are a relatively recent development. Such plays, along with poetry and fiction, emerged first in French-speaking countries, starting in the 1930s. Literature in English experienced a marked explosion beginning in the 1950s.

We tend to forget how huge a continent Africa is, with a quarter of the world's land area. African culture, therefore, is far from monolithic, varying widely from country to country, and from tribe to tribe.

---

[*] Shakespeare, *Coriolanus*

In the past seven decades or so there have arisen at least 150 playwrights of repute.

Of these about half have employed the English language. A major boost to theatrical activity in Africa has come from the establishment of many universities since World War II and the achievement of political independence by nearly fifty countries since 1951.

One particularly productive area has been South Africa, with some two dozen significant black playwrights. A second has been West Africa—notably Nigeria and Ghana. Nigeria, with its enormous population (around 136 million), its new universities, and its rich Yoruba traditions, has given us some two dozen noteworthy playwrights. Ghana (21 million), with a half dozen universities, has spawned some ten respected dramatists.

Out of all the African playwrights, two have so far attained the status of major world figures. One is the prolific white South African dramatist Athol Fugard (born 1932), some of whose work has been created jointly with two formidable black actors, John Kani (b. 1943) and Winston Ntshona (b. 1941)—all active in the early 1960s with the Johannesburg troupe called the Serpent Players. The other is the black Nigerian writer Wole Soyinka (b. 1934)—also noted as poet, novelist and memoirist—who in 1986 became the first African to receive the Nobel Prize in Literature.

The other West African nations have by no means been theatrically silent. Nabie Yayah Swaray (b. 1953), author of *Worl' Do For Fraid*, is a native of Sierra Leone, which has a small area of only 28,000 square miles and a population of six million. Swaray is a successor to several older Sierra Leonean anglophone playwrights.

John Joseph Akar (1927-75) was a major cultural figure, heading the Sierra Leone Broadcasting Service (1957-67), founding the National Dance Troupe (1963), and composing the music for the national anthem ("High we exalt thee," words by C. Nelson Fyle) adopted when the country became independent of Britain in April of 1961. He wrote several plays, including *Valley Without Echo* (1957), one of the first African dramas to be performed in Europe, and the prize-winning *Cry Tamba* (1961).

Of historical importance were the two plays written by the physician R[aymond] Sarif Easmon (1913-97), both imitative of upper-class British drawing-room comedies. The first, which won a prize, was *Dear Parent and Ogre* (1961), a rather amateurish and pretentious work. *The New Patriots* (1965) was a considerable improvement in structure if too preachy.

Much more accomplished is Yulisa "Pat" Amadu Maddy (b. 1936), who has written more than a dozen plays, with an emphasis on ordinary citizens. Like Swaray, Maddy often provides music in his printed editions: *Alla Gbah* (1967), *Gbana-Bendu* (1971), *Obasai* (1971), and the prison drama *Yon-Kon* (1971). Among his other works are the radio play *If Wishes Were Horses* (1963), *Big Breeze Blow* (1974), and *Journey Into Christmas* (1980). In 1977 he was arrested by the government and for some time went into exile in Denmark.

Gaston Bart-Williams (b. 1938), the founder in 1958 of the African Youth Cultural Society, is the author of several dra-

135

mas, including three plays for West German Radio, *In Praise of Madness* (1968), *Uhuru* (1969), and the experimental, somewhat Joycean *The Drug* (1972).

Sierra Leone contains some twenty ethnic groups with their own languages, of which Mende and Temne are the most widespread. Although English is the country's official tongue, the Krio language serves as the lingua franca.

A pioneer was Thomas Decker (1916-78), who translated Shakespeare's *Julius Caesar* into Krio as *Juliohs Siza* (1964), followed by *As You Like It* with the title *Udat di Kiap Fit*. So successful were the Sierra Leone stagings that they inspired the writing of original plays in Krio—notably three by Juliana John [now Rowe] (b.1938): *Na Mammy Born Am* (1968), *I Dey I Noh Du* (1969), and *I Don Reach Tem*.

[Raymond] Dele Charley (1948-94), co-founder in 1968 of the Tabule Experimental Theatre, wrote plays in both English (the much lauded *Blood of the Stranger*, 1977) and Krio (*Petikot Kohna*, 1982). The sadly short-lived John Kolosa Kargbo (1954-94), co-founder in 1973 of the Songhai Theatre, also wrote bilingually. Police tried to keep audiences away from his *Let Me Die Alone* (1979). In the same year his *Poyoh Ton Wahala* resulted in his arrest and a banning of the play, an attack on corruption in high places. The government also banned two later plays, *Case of the Pregnant Schoolgirl* and *Ekundayo*. Lawrence Quaku-Woode (b.1950), founder in 1974 of the Balangi Tiata, ambitiously operates on several levels in his *God Pas Konsibul* (published 1988).

136

One scholar (Chris Corcoran) who had spent considerable time in Sierra Leone reported in 1990 that she had gathered the names (and usually texts) of 327 English and Krio plays by 108 playwrights. She added that there were then 64 functioning drama groups, about half of them in the capital city of Freetown.

It was in Kambia Town in the north that Nabie Swaray was born. His involvement in the theatre started early, since he was already acting in pantomime at the age of four. His interest continued during his school years; and in the fall of 1975, during his freshman year at Harvard College, there was a reading of his first play, *Dance of the Witches*. Early in 1976 he began work on *The Drums of Death*, which he retitled *Worl' Do For Fraid*. This second play received a public reading at Harvard in 1978, a fully staged production in Boston in 1980, and, after some revision, was offered at Harvard again in 1984. Since embarking on this work, Swaray has written many more plays, some with African content and some without any at all.

Worl' Do For Fraid, which is set in the Sierra Leone of 1950, is a highly effective piece and one rich in content. One of the themes explored is the conflict of religious beliefs. Another is the extreme behavior of men greedy for political power, who indulge in ritual murder and rape to gain their ends. A third is the traumatic return to one's native habitat after lengthy sojourn and education in a distant and different cultural environment. All three of these subjects crop up frequently in African plays and novels; but they permit a wide variety of changes to be rung upon them, so that gifted writers can return to them again and again with success.

137

The most influential treatment of these themes is the cycle of four Nigerian novels by Chinua Achebe (b. 1930) that appeared from 1958 to 1966. The first of this tetralogy, *Things Fall Apart*, although not the earliest anglophone work of fiction from West Africa, is the quintessential, archetypal African novel, occupying a position comparable to that of *Huckleberry Finn* in American literature.

The clash of traditional religion and colonial Christianity is dealt with by writers in other countries, such as the adjacent Cameroun, which produced Kenjo Jumbam's story of a boy's growing up, *The White Man of God* (1980). Swaray's countryman William Conton wrote *The African* (1960), whose hero (Kisimi Kamara) receives his education in England and then goes back to Africa. Lenrie Peters' partly autobiographical *The Second Round* (1965), although written by a Gambian (whose parents were natives of Sierra Leone), tells the tale of a young Sierra Leonean named Kawa who attends medical school in England and after some years returns to his native country.

This brings us back to Swaray's play, in which Abass, trained in medicine and psychiatry during a decade in London, comes back to his family village in Sierra Leone. But with all his modern European education, Abass discovers that he is unable to deal with the conditions he finds at home. Like many other African writers, Swaray feels that it is too simple just to blame the whites and their colonialism for society's ills. This might have been valid in the Republic of South Africa, with its loathesome entrenchment of *apartheid* from the 1948 election until 1994; elsewhere, however, the situation has been more complex.

But ritual murder, rape, and the forced drinking of blood? Westerners may think this far-fetched, and feel like Judge Brack, who, when Ibsen's Hedda Gabler shoots herself in the temple, exclaims, "Good God, people don't *do* things like that!" But Ibsen's point is that people *do* behave that way. And when one examines the history of many African nations, one sees that the coming of independence has not been an unmixed blessing, to put it mildly. Recent years have seen numerous instances of assassinations, coups d'état, countercoups, voting fraud, bribery and others kinds of corruption. Sierra Leone, in fact, has been particularly plagued with such turbulence and instability, including a civil war from 1991 to 2002.

At one point in *Worl' Do For Fraid*, Abass tells his mother, "The white people believe in hard work. They believe in themselves—we black people don't. White people worship work! But *we* are taught to hate work; to fear life and love death." One actor who had been cast to play Abass refused to say these lines; and when Swaray, believing them true to Abass' character, insisted on retaining the speech, the actor quit the role.

In this play Swaray is clearly indicting his country. But he does so to a considerable extent through allegory, implication, and indirection. It is useful to compare his approach with that of another Harvard-trained West African writer, Ayi Kwei Armah (b. 1939). Armah saw his native Ghana as similarly infected with sickness and corruption, and conveyed his disgust in his first two stunning novels, *The Beautyful Ones Are Not Yet Born* (1968) and *Fragments* (1970). In the latter there is even a protagonist, Baako, who, like Abass, returns home from several years of foreign study (this time it's in the United States), and is so horrified that he eventually goes mad. Armah writes of his country in the most harsh and savage terms. Images of excrement and putrefaction and slime are ubiquitous. Armah wants to turn the reader's stomach, and rub his nose in the stench. There is more than one way to achieve the same end.

While traditional religion and Christianity are both present in *Worl' Do For Fraid*, Swaray has also included Islam in the mix. This is perfectly justified, since a number of African nations have a substantial proportion of Muslims. In the past few decades, the breakdown in Sierra Leone has been something on the order of 10 percent Christian, 60 percent Muslim, and 30 percent traditional (often described as animist). These are not always necessarily mutually exclusive. Swaray's own father was a Muslim *imam*, but his mother found no difficulty in practicing a combination of Islam and animism.

Christianity is represented by Pastor Brown, a Protestant clergyman who is a friend of Abass' Muslim father, Baimbadi. But traditional beliefs occupy the largest part of the play—and these are of course especially instructive to Westerners. We find polygyny, witchcraft, herb medicine, and spirit possession, along with the prophetic power of dreams (oneiromancy), of birds (ornithomancy), and of snakes (ophiomancy). The ghost of the murdered wife puts in a vocal appearance, like the ghost of Hamlet's father. And there are special ceremonial practices and garments. In addition to occasional songs, from time to time we have the *tabule*, a large ominous-sounding drum; a transverse bamboo flute; and, at the wedding ceremony, the *balangi*, a xylophone with gourd resonators.

Swaray is careful to differentiate his various characters' mode of speech. Pastor Brown, for example, is fond of invoking maxims: "Fortune and misfortune are man's closest neighbors"; "All roads have curves"; "When the tallest tree in the bush falls, all the little ones will wither away." And Pabuya, the colorful and delightful market-sweeper, talks in unsophisticated dialect (which provides the play's title).

Worl' Do For Fraid is a play of many facets and many layers. One might put it beside *The Black Hermit* (1962), a much-admired drama by the Kenyan writer James T. Ngugi (b. 1938), who took the name Ngugi wa Thiong'o. This work too has a Christian pastor and a protagonist (Remi) who has been educated in a large city and eventually returns to his tribal village with a view to righting its ills. Next to Swaray's play Ngugi's effort seems rather simplistic and amateurish. *Worl' Do For Fraid* is the real article—a skillfully wrought and eminently stageworthy work that also insightfully opens up a fascinating world that is unknown territory to most of us.

Caldwell Titcomb is professor emeritus at Brandeis University and a charter member of the American Theatre Critics Association.

Transcription and Translations of the Songs

PASTOR BROWN
[ACT 1, SCENE 2]

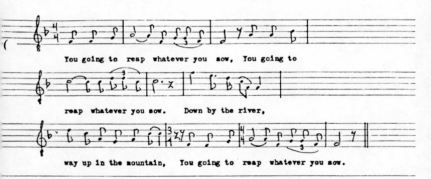

You going to reap whatever you sow, You going to reap whatever you sow. Down by the river, way up in the mountain, You going to reap whatever you sow.

THE SONG ABOUT BOMSOKO,
THE UNSYMPATHETIC CREDITOR
[ACT 1, SCENE 3: PABUYA]

Maienkayray! Maienkayray!
I say bitter,
bitter, bitter, bitter, bitter, but getting very bitter indeed!
"Hassan!"
"—Yes!
Whoever owes me money, must come and pay!
I am tormented by Bomsoko, by what I owe her.
Oh woe! Woe-oh, woe-oh. Maienkayray!

Today I've got some really terrible trouble—
But getting even worse! Oh, woe.
But—now it all does not bother me so much.
Today I've got some really terrible trouble—
But getting even worse! Oh, woe.
But—now it all does not bother me so much.

Oh woe! Woe-woe-oh, woe-oh!
Right away you see it floating,
[—her vagina that she so misused—]
which tells it's been made worthless.
Oh woe! woe-oh, woe-oh!
Oh woe! woe-oh, woe-oh. Maienkayray!

p
x = inflected speech, not precise pitch

"Maienkayray! Maienkayray! Ee yaw k'thuma, k'thuma, k'thuma, k'-

'thuma, k'thuma, kere day keet! Asana!" "Na!" "Aw - way me ba k'-

ruhn, to woor - ay! Boasowkaw, aw po mee ketha, Ee yaw, "Woyo, woyo,

Maienkay-ray!" Ee sawthaw thaw-naw uhngyeek thawn-pay. Kere day

keet. Ee vowye Ee bawthayrye saw, kere day keet. Ee yaw,

woyo, woyo! Ng na gbothawng, kuh foyay, Pa gbothawng, kuh con-

demn! Ee yaw, woyo, wo-yo, wo - yo! Ee yaw, woyo, wo-

yo, Maienkay-ray!

145

FIRE, FIRE, FIRE
[ACT 1, SCENE 3: PABUYA,
LATER SUNG BY DRISSA]

Fire, fire, fire mama, Fire, dey cam. Fire, fire, fire

mama, Fire dey cam. I want to see my loving wife,

Loving wife I love so well. Fire, fire, fire baby-yoh! Fire dey

cam. Pompo-di! Kiddi pom-po! Pompo-di! Kiddi pom-po!

Pabuya ends
here. Drissa
proceeds to end.

(

SWEETIE PALM WINE
[ACT 1, SCENE 3: PABUYA]

Wherever I go, city palm wine dey wait for me. I

board a bus to Lum'ly, I met a bus con - ductor.

Five shillings be charged me For sak' of my edu-cation.

Boys and girls were laughing, They say I was a drunkard,

But I am a free-born, And Freetown is my colony!

Everywhere I go, city palm wine dey wait for me.

THE SONG OF THE DOE RESCUED BY THE WOMEN
[ACT II, SCENE 1: NENE]

We are fed up with this affair of the doe the men wanted to kill.
It's been going on for a long time now.
When the doe came into Dibiya,
We sent for the chiefs to settle this affair.
Oh! We also had to send for Almamie Sorie.

The chiefs had to tell the men:
"Leave the women alone in this affair."
—We women have suffered long.

When the doe ran into our backyard
Where we the women were cooking,
There we trapped it.
The chief's dog came and warned them not to kill it.
"Stop it!" said the dog. "This doe must not be killed!
It belongs to no one.
If you kill it, you'll get in a lot of trouble."
Now we're fed up with all this talk
About the doe that we the women rescued.
This nonsense has been going on for a long time now.

Uhngpa wawr uh buhkee su! Uh-wonee me kanay mu. Uhng pa wawr uh

buhkee su. Uhngpa wawr muhng wong de Deebeeyah, Ta

sawara angbai a-kande. A day pa su t' t' k-aw. Oh, yayow, Almamee So-

rie. Ta kanay anglang-gbah: "Tung tayow! Oh, tan-tays

eppahye!" S'bow rah k-mambuhrah. Aw-war maw woor ro ruhrayn gay,

Ruh boanga ang tang khhkaw. Uhngt'n ka kanday dayray,

Taw pa, "Gbuhpe! Moontha ba kaw, Ng t'kuhruh eppah."

Uhngpa wawr uh buhkee su! Uhwonee me kanay mu. Uhngpa wawr uh

buhkee su!

149

THE SONG OF LOVE AND THE WORLD
[ACT III, SCENE 1: PABUYA]

The world is finished: we've lost our world—
Don't tell me how sweet the world is.
So if you think it's sweet because you're flirting with a woman
Why, go ahead and flirt!
But—don't tell me how sweet the world is:
Not all the world is sweet, not all of life is easy love.

Hurray, hurray, hurray!
Hurry, hurray, hurray!

Oh yes, mama, that's how it is!
Oh yes, mama, that's how it is!

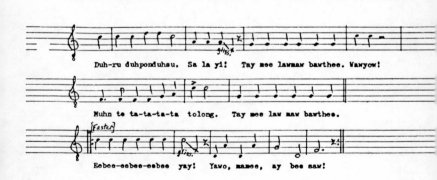

Duh-ru duhponduhsu. Sa la yi! Tay mee lawmaw bawthee. Wawyow!

Muhn te ta-ta-ta-ta tolong. Tay mee law maw bawthee.

Eebee-eebee-eebee yay! Yawo, mamee, ay bee saw!

150

EEMA YELLI-OH!
[ACT III, SCENE 1: GODMAMY & CROWD]

Eema Yelli - oh!   Eema Yelli te-te!

Eema Yelli - bah!   Eema Yelli te-te!

Eebee, eebee yay!

THE SONG OF THE BEAUTIFUL YOUNG GIRL WHO
DIES UNMARRIED.
[ACT III, SCENE 2: FATIMAH]

I will not cry anymore,
I will not cry because I'm dying unmarried,
Because I'm dying unmarried.
Oh! Yenkin.

On the way to Mayefa
I found a plum,
I found a pure, innocent plum, oh Yenkin.

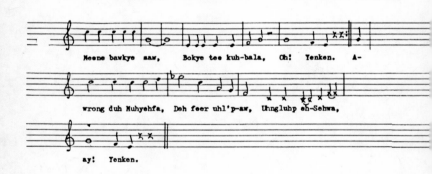

Meene bawkye aaw, Bokye tee kuh-bala, Oh! Yenken. A-

wrong duh Muhyehfa, Deh feer uhl'p-aw, Uhngluhp eh-Sehwa,

ay! Yenken.

THE SONG OF THE CHAMELEON
AND THE LEOPARD
[ACT III, SCENE 2, FATIMAH]

Which way should I take, Chameleon, with your wagging
tail—
Tailwagger, tailwagger.
Father Leopard, allow me the way—
Tailwagger, tailwagger.

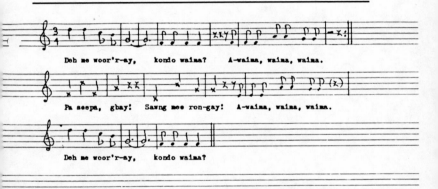

Deh me woor'r-ay,   kondo waima?   A-waima, waima, waima.

Pa seepa, gbay! Sawng mee ron-gay! A-waima, waima, waima.

Deh me woor'r-ay,   kondo waima?

[Songs transcribed by Caldwell Titcomb from
the singing of the playwright]

153